GROWING PAINS

JOHN LOREN & PAULA SANDFORD

Charisma
HOUSE
A STRANG COMPANY

Most STRANG COMMUNICATIONS/CHARISMA HOUSE/SILOAM/
FRONTLINE/REALMS/EXCEL BOOKS products are available at special
quantity discounts for bulk purchase for sales promotions, premiums,
fund-raising, and educational needs. For details, write Strang
Communications/Charisma House/Siloam/FrontLine/Realms/Excel
Books, 600 Rinehart Road, Lake Mary, Florida 32746, or telephone (407)
333-0600.

GROWING PAINS by John Loren and Paula Sandford
Published by Charisma House
A Strang Company
600 Rinehart Road
Lake Mary, Florida 32746
www.charismahouse.com

Unless otherwise noted, all Scripture quotations are from the New
American Standard Bible. Copyright © 1960, 1962, 1963, 1968, 1971, 1972,
1973, 1975, 1977 by the Lockman Foundation. Used by permission. (www
.Lockman.org).

Scripture quotations marked AMP are from the Amplified Bible. Old
Testament copyright © 1965, 1987 by the Zondervan Corporation. The
Amplified New Testament copyright © 1954, 1958, 1987 by the Lockman
Foundation. Used by permission.

Scripture quotations marked KJV are from the King James Version of the
Bible.

Scripture quotations marked NIV are from the Holy Bible, New
International Version. Copyright © 1973, 1978, 1984, International Bible
Society. Used by permission.

Scripture quotations marked NRSV are from the New Revised Standard
Version of the Bible. Copyright © 1989 by the Division of Christian Education

Cover Designer: Justin Evans
Design Director: Bill Johnson

Library of Congress Cataloging-in-Publication Data

Loren, John.
Growing pains / John Loren and Paula Sandford.
    p. cm.
  ISBN 978-1-59979-278-1
1. Suffering--Religious aspects--Christianity. 2. Adjustment (Psychology)--Religious aspects--Christianity. 3. Child rearing--Religious aspects--Christianity. 4. Suffering in children. 5. Adjustment (Psychology) in children. I. Sandford, Paula. II. Title.
  BV4909.L57 2008
  248.4--dc22
                                    2007051321

Some people and incidents in this book are composites created by the authors from their experiences as ministers. Names and details have been changed, and any similarity between the names and stories of individuals described in this book known to readers is purely coincidental.

Portions of this book were previously published as *The Transformation of the Inner Man* by John and Paula Sandford, copyright © 1982 by Victory House, Inc., ISBN 0-932081-13-4; and *Healing the Wounded Spirit* by John and Paula Sandford, copyright © 1985 by Victory House, Inc., ISBN 0-932081-14-2.

08 09 10 11 12 — 987654321
Printed in the United States of America

This book is lovingly dedicated to Mark and Maureen Sandford. Our son Mark is the spiritual director of Elijah House Ministries and, as such, has spent countless hours editing everything Paula and I and everyone at Elijah House has written, including this book, protecting us from error, misspoken statements, and misquoted biblical references. His genius has been lifesaving for all of us. Maureen, his lovely wife, stands beside him in ministry.

ACKNOWLEDGMENTS

Our first acknowledgment is to the Holy Spirit of our Lord Jesus Christ. Countless times when we were stuck, unable to find the keys of knowledge that would locate bad roots—and good—in individuals' hearts, the Holy Spirit revealed the secrets of men's hearts (Ps. 44:21; 1 Cor. 14:25). We were then able to apply the blood, cross, and resurrection of Jesus Christ accurately to set people free. Many of those revelations became the keys of knowledge presented in this and our other books.

We also want to acknowledge the patient tolerance of our six children, who not only had to sometimes endure late suppers and absentminded parents, but also became fond of saying, "Our dirty linen is hung out for all the world to see!" as with their permission, their foibles and problems became written testimonies. If the Holy Spirit has been our teacher, our children have often been the classroom. Fortunately, they all loved it and have become strong, devout Christians, serving the Lord faithfully.

And how could we have served and written had not our board and staff at Elijah House supported us, prayed intercessorily, and loved us when we were at our most unlovable? Our thanks to them, and finally to all the editors and other servants at Charisma House, who labored to make our writings accessible and understandable to all Christians—and hopefully, to some non-Christians, who may find healing and, more hopefully yet, rebirth in our Lord as they read.

CONTENTS

INTRODUCTION

Paula and I have been amazed at the rapid maturation of the body of Christ in the last twenty-five years or so. What would have fallen then on deaf or misunderstanding ears is now easily understood and received. In teaching, we would sometimes begin a biblical quote and put a hand to an ear to signify the congregation should finish the quote, and whereas years ago what followed was a resounding silence, now, audiences finish the quote in unison. Inner healing, which used to receive critical aversion, now is hungrily received. Worship has become lively and from the heart rather than mere rote. Men, who used to be conspicuous by their absence from worship and Bible study, are now increasingly not only present but also assuming leadership roles. Our Lord is moving to prepare His bride for His return. For all this we give hearty thanks, reveling to be alive and given second birth and the gifts of the Holy Spirit in this wondrous time in the Church's history.

But we are equally amazed and appalled at the lack of maturity and integrity in some in the body of Christ, especially among some of the leadership. Reports of fallen leaders have become so frequent as to be almost commonplace! We are shamed and grieved before our forgiving and loving Lord. His gracious forgiveness is often being presumed upon and His name shamed before His people and the world. We wonder, as does the world,

1

how can men and women who profess to love Him, and who have been raised to high places of service, so callously, it seems, depart from respecting the holiness He calls for and succumb to sins they never should have entertained?

Our recently republished book *Why Good People Mess Up* is an attempt to stem the tide, as are our first three books in the Transformation Series—*Transforming the Inner Man, God's Power to Change*, and *Letting Go of Your Past*. This book, *Growing Pains*, is the fourth and last in that series, all designed to free, transform, and mature Christians for holy and righteous living in Christ.

What has been happening is that ever since the Holy Spirit began to fall on mankind in the Azusa Street revival of 1906, men and women have been equipped, as prophesied in Joel 2:28, with the nine gifts of the Holy Spirit. Scripture says, "A man's gift makes room for him" (Prov. 18:16). Consequently, men and women have been rather quickly elevated to places of high service—apostles, prophets, evangelists, pastors, and teachers (Eph. 4:11), plus miracle workers, healers, exorcists, and so on. This is good, but there is a rather comic expression found in Acts 9:29–30. Saul (who became the great apostle Paul) had been persecuting the Church, but then he was radically converted and went about confounding the Hellenistic Jews and "speaking out boldly in the name of the Lord" (v. 28). Then comes the humorous statement (for those who have eyes to see it): "But when the brethren learned of it, they brought him down to Caesarea and sent him away to Tarsus. So the church throughout all Judea and Galilee and Samaria enjoyed peace" (vv. 30–31). I think maybe after each of us is first converted, we ought to be sent off for a while to our own "Tarsus" so the church might have great peace. There at Tarsus, in eleven years of the Holy Spirit's working on Saul, He transformed a hate-filled, legalistic Pharisee into the compassionate lover of God and mankind who became the great apostle Paul, by whom most of the letters of the New Testament were written.

Having ministered to many leaders who have fallen, I can testify that none who fell, at least, those to whom I have ministered, have had their eleven years at Tarsus. Paul wrote, "Do not lay hands upon anyone too hastily and thus share responsibility for the sins of others; keep yourself free from sin" (1 Tim. 5:22). Since this verse is in the context of a discussion about elders, Paul was not speaking of general prayers to bestow the Holy Spirit, but was advising not to lay hands to elevate men or women to positions of high service too soon; their errors and sins, due to immaturity and undealt-with sinful character structures, would redound to the harm of those who laid hands on too soon. But so many today are too quickly elevated, not having received ministry to deal with malformations in their character. We believe that our books, listed above, should be prerequisites before men and women are allowed to serve in high places. Before his death, Jamie Buckingham, having read the first edition of *Why Good People Mess Up* (then titled *Why Some Christians Commit Adultery*), declared that no pastor should be let out of seminary without that book having been required reading!

But it is not merely leaders who need their eleven years and who have been falling morally and in other ways. The rank and file of Christians everywhere is no different. All desperately need to have the wounds and resultant coping practices that were formed in childhood dealt with by the blood and cross of Jesus.

That is the aim of this book—and of the entire Transformation Series. Christians simply must learn how to apply the blood, cross, and resurrection life of Jesus to everything in their lives after they have received Him as their Lord and Savior. In this book you will find lessons on how we were formed and how to transform whatever has been malformed. The chapters teach how to minister to our hearts as we have progressed through our lives, from our first prenatal reactions, through nursing and toddler times, up through our childhood years, and on into adulthood. You will learn of the powerful negative effects of many character flaws, such as inner vows and hearts of stone, and how to be set free and heal others.

The book should become a valuable reference volume to be mined regularly when problems arise in your own life or in the lives of those for whom you yearn and pray: "What was that answer I saw for this problem? Oh, here it is. That started prenatally, and here's how to heal it."

We don't have to grieve helplessly as our relatives and friends in Christ stumble or merely live lives far below the blessedness God intends. There are simple, profound, and wise answers, ways to minister that really work.

Read on—but put to work what you learn.

CHAPTER 1

LIFE BEGINS IN THE WOMB

Yet Thou art He who didst bring me forth from the womb;
Thou didst make me trust when upon my mother's breasts.
Upon Thee I was cast from birth; Thou hast been my God
from my mother's womb.

—PSALM 22:9

In Luke 4:18 Jesus said, "He hath sent me to *heal* the brokenhearted" (KJV, emphasis added). Many new adoptive parents, while well prepared and eager to love and nurture their long-awaited child and to provide bountifully for him or her, have not at all comprehended how deep and intense the brokenheartedness in that little one can be. They may have good, solid faith in the power of the Lord to bless and heal. But without instruction about what to do, their love can fall short of penetrating the spirit of their child and thus fail to effect real healing.

Many parents, natural and adoptive, have come to us saying, "I know that my baby needs affection, and I *want* to hold him and rock him, but he won't let me. He stiffens in my arms." Or, "My toddler seems to want comfort and love and will come crying to me, but when I pick her up she pushes me away." Some others may report, "This child is insatiable. He has to be held *all* the time; he can never get enough." We hear of older children putting their parents through endless rounds of testing, as if to say, "If I do this, will you still love me?" They will reject before they can be rejected, attempt to punish their parents by failure to achieve, or go to the other extreme and strive to please. When they do please, they are often not able to come to rest in the sincere affirmation of family and teachers. They may refuse affection and then project onto parents, who have given consistent unconditional love, the accusation, "You don't love me." Such children may steal items they have no need of simply to get attention or to express some unidentified sense of having been robbed themselves and their need to retaliate or fill the emptiness. They may lie for no explicable reason and to effect no practical purpose. Facing such actions, parents may cry out in desperation, "Where did we go wrong? Maybe we weren't cut out to be parents."

They need to know that all such attitudes and behaviors, especially in adopted children, can be summed up as the message in Psalm 109:22: "I am afflicted and needy, and my heart is wounded within me." Adoptive parents need to realize that their child came to them deeply wounded and that they should not regard manifestations of that woundedness as conclusive evidence of their failure as parents. As natural parents become aware, they should willingly and without self-condemnation accept responsibility for those wounding circumstances, attitudes, and actions that were present in their lives to afflict their children from the time of their conception. This does not mean endless painful bearing of guilt. Forgiveness follows repentance. Neither does it mean that parents have to resign themselves to hopelessness. The brokenhearted can be healed, and the depth of their woundedness can become the strength of their compassion and sensitivity for others.

First there is a need for parents to understand something of the origin, nature, and functions of a person's personal spirit.

> But there is [a vital force] a spirit [of intelligence] in man, and the breath of the Almighty gives men understanding.
> —JOB 32:8, AMP

As we mature, we interpret experiences with our mind, but before we have a developed intellect with which to reason, we have a mind in the spirit within us. As soon as we begin to form within the womb, that breath from God, which is the core of our essence, is breathed into us, or we would not have life at all.

> . . . the body without the spirit is dead.
> —JAMES 2:26

Our spirit, according to the Word of God, is capable of experiencing and expressing many things: for example, troubledness (John 13:21), distress (Acts 17:16), and belonging (Rom. 8:16–17). Our spirit testifies (Rom. 8:16–17), prays (1 Cor. 14:14), sings (1 Cor. 14:15), praises God (1 Cor. 14:16), tends toward envy (James 4:5), expresses faithfulness or unfaithfulness (Ps. 78:8), and worships (John 4:23). In Luke 1:41–44, as soon as the sound of Elizabeth's greeting reached Mary's ears, the baby (John the Baptist) leaped in her womb for joy! Since John could not see Jesus, his spirit had to have sensed His presence.

Scripture tells us that we sin in our spirit:

> And in whose spirit there is not deceit!
>
> —PSALM 32:2

> Create in me a clean heart, O God, and renew a steadfast spirit within me.
>
> —PSALM 51:10

> I will give you a new heart and put a new spirit within you; and I will remove the heart of stone from your flesh and give you a heart of flesh. And I will put My Spirit within you.
>
> —EZEKIEL 36:26–27

> Let us cleanse ourselves from all defilement of flesh and spirit.
>
> —2 CORINTHIANS 7:1

Remember that Jesus said, "There is nothing outside the man which going into him can defile him; but the things which proceed out of the man are what defile the man" (Mark 7:15). Second Corinthians 7:1 is not talking about soiling one's spirit from without, but sin coming from within.

That sinning in our spirit begins at our very beginnings:

> The wicked are estranged from the womb; these who speak lies go astray from birth.
>
> —PSALM 58:3

> I knew that you would deal very treacherously; and you have been called a rebel from birth.
>
> —ISAIAH 48:8

In the womb, every adoptive child has experienced rejection from his natural parents. He has absorbed in his spirit all the elements of his environment: the fear, tension, uncertainty, anxiety, guilt, shame, confusion, hatred, anger, and pain of his mother. He lacks the security of being invited, nurtured, supported in love, and welcomed into the world. Before he sees the light of this earth he may be confused already about his identity, his right to live, his belonging. He may already have a sense that "something must be wrong with me or my parents would not feel the way they do." Can it be that while in the womb a child can already be bound with lies? "I'm ugly, unlovable." "I'm a burden, a threat, a mistake." "I'm no good." "No one will receive me." Can it be that while in the womb he may already be reacting in his spirit with resentment, tightening up in defensiveness, punishing with aggressive anger, or withdrawing in fear or rebellion against life? Certainly rest and trust are neither born nor formed in him. Perhaps the same wounding experiences and reactions may be registered in the heart of a child whose natural parents decide to keep him, except less potently because of not being given away. *given away for 1st 8 yrs. of life*

Can issues that beset adults have had their origins in the womb? John and I have come to believe that they can. We discovered insights into the awareness and capacity of a child to react in utero simply by the inspiration of the Holy Spirit over many years of prayer ministry (and in the process of raising our own six children). We ministered as the Lord directed and were gratified to find our perceptions and prayers confirmed by changes in the behavior of the people to whom we ministered. We have been delighted to see our findings and experiences increasingly confirmed by medical research.

All this raises some serious biblical questions. Can a child commit sins while in the womb? How can he even be capable of making such choices? If he is capable of sinning, would a just

God hold him accountable for them? These questions are not to be treated lightly. After we review the medical research, we will talk about how these and related questions should be answered. Then we will discuss how we should apply the research in a biblical way to our lives and the lives of our children.

Since the 1981 publication of Dr. Thomas Verny's book *The Secret Life of the Unborn Child*,[1] interest in the prenatal has risen exponentially. The volume of material is too extensive to record here. I suggest that you go to your computer to Google and search the phrase "prenatal research." You will find lists of articles, dozens to the page, on the prenatal effects of alcohol, drugs, smoking, medications, and supplements on autism and other conditions, as well as articles about how the attitudes and actions of expectant parents affect children for many years beyond their birth. You will find many articles on "belly talk," advocating how to communicate with a baby in utero, how such communicating with babies in utero helps motor skills and abilities to relate to others postpartum, and so on.

Not too many years ago, when Paula and I first wrote about the prenatal from our Christian prayer ministry perspective, we were met by many Christians with scoffing and attack. And many in the medical field contested Dr. Verny's research and consequent statements. Very little positive research could be found to corroborate. Since then, attitudes and reactions have almost entirely reversed! You will find such copious material, from highly respected scholarly sources, as to feel that it has become nearly overwhelming.

The existence of stimuli and reactions in the experiences of babies in utero is now no longer questioned by informed scholars.

The questions now are: What does this mean in parental behaviors? In affecting pregnant women's prenatal diets and behaviors? How should fathers relate not only to prospective mothers but also to their unborn children? And the questions continue.

We look forward to the day when sociologists and psychologists will have perfected consistent mature theories of child rearing that include major teachings on how parental behavior affects prenatal children and therefore should be adapted for healthy, wholesome child raising. Many articles now report on "belly talk." Belly talk is defined as speaking to one's baby in utero and expecting the baby to be beneficially affected. An article titled "An Open Window to the World" goes into further detail about this phenomenon:

> The core idea of this technique is to encourage parents to learn the potential of their unborn child during gestation and postpartum development. [It] was not made just to increase intellectual results but to conceive an emotional [sic], mental [sic], and socially developed human being.[2]

Another article talks about prenatal stimulation through *music*.[3] The article discusses the beneficial effects of good music on babies in utero—citing accelerated developmental skills and abilities and reading at an accelerated rate, stating that most can play music by age four and a half and that all do so by age five and a half. It affirms that these same children read, transpose, and compose music in first grade! The article goes on to say:

> Prenatal research indicates that your baby in utero is an emotionally aware, spiritually aware, physical person with all of his/her senses actively functioning long before birth. Scientific research shows that you have an awesome opportunity to affect

your child's destiny, development, preference and personality by carefully guarding and creating an enhanced prenatal
environment.[4]

These studies concur that the baby in the womb hears, tastes,
feels, and learns, and that *what* he thus experiences begins to
shape his attitudes and expectations about himself. He can sense
and react not only to large undifferentiated emotions in the
mother like love and hate, but also to shaded emotions such as
ambivalence and ambiguity.

Studies reveal that a child in utero manifests tastes in music,
responding calmly to composers such as Vivaldi and Mozart,
but reacting with violent motions to the more pounding perfor-
mances of Beethoven and to all kinds of rock music.[5] While still
in the womb, the baby learns to recognize his father's voice and
to be comforted by quiet soothing tones that reassure. Within
an hour and a half of delivery, the baby can pick out his father's
voice and respond to it emotionally.[6] Quarreling of parents while
the child is in the womb tends to produce fearful, jumpy, under-
sized, timid, and inordinately emotionally dependent children.[7]

A chronic state of uncertainty, fear, and deep-seated anxiety
is built into a child in utero whose mother smokes, and he will
react when his mother even *thinks* of having a cigarette![8] In his
book, Dr. Verny related numerous fascinating stories of prenatal
memory and many case histories in which the doctors concluded
that in some way the child made decisions to react, such as refusal
to bond with the mother after birth because of her refusal to bond
with the child before delivery. He reported the formation of attitudes and personality traits as a result of prenatal or birth trauma.
The book says nothing of spirit, documenting only that which can

be observed and evaluated clinically from a secular point of view and offering many hypotheses for which there is growing evidence. The author suggested love as a powerful force for healing.

A friend of ours who was a pediatric nurse for many years told us that she had learned to see a direct correlation between newborn babies' refusal to nurse and the attitude of one or both of the parents. Searching out answers, she had discovered that in such cases some sort of rejection of the baby was present during pregnancy. "Often," she said, "the baby will turn away from the embrace of the parent who did not wholeheartedly welcome him while he was in the womb, even though that parent may have welcomed him after birth." She described extreme anger in many newborns and told us that, in talking with the mothers, she has discovered that the baby's father had left, the mother had experienced sex with many partners and had no husband, the baby was the product of an affair, or the mother had simply hated being pregnant.

BIBLICAL BASIS FOR PRENATAL SIN

Now back to those biblical questions we raised earlier. Can a child sin in the womb? How can he even be capable of making such choices? If he is capable of sinning, would a just God hold him accountable?

There are those who claim that no child can sin at all until the age of thirteen. That is the "age of accountability," based on the Jewish practice of the bar mitzvah, the coming of age ceremony for boys (for girls it is called bat mitzvah). At thirteen, a child was no longer primarily accountable to his parents; he was now accountable to the Law (and thus to God).

However, Scripture nowhere identifies thirteen as the age of accountability. That is not to say there is none. It may vary widely, from earlier than usual for a bright child to not at all for a severely mentally handicapped person. In any case, "age of accountability" never meant that children can't sin. It only means that before that age, they are not yet held accountable in the same way adults are, for they do not yet possess an adult understanding of the Law. But Scripture clearly states that children can and do sin: "It is by his deeds that a lad distinguishes himself if his conduct is pure and right" (Prov. 20:11). Psalm 58:3 says, "The wicked are estranged from the womb; these who speak lies go astray from birth."

Even when faced with these verses, some still doubt that an unborn child or even a young child can sin, for they think all sin is conscious and deliberate. How, they ask, can a child so young make these kinds of decisions? But Scripture says even adults can sin unintentionally: "If a person *sins unintentionally* in any of the things which the LORD has commanded not to be done, and commits any of them... [later context says a sacrifice must be made for that sin]" (Lev. 4:2, emphasis added). This is true not only for those who understand the Law. Persons who don't know the Law (including children too young to understand it) are also lawbreakers: "For *all who have sinned without the Law* will also perish without the Law; and all who have sinned under the Law will be judged by the Law" (Rom. 2:12, emphasis added).

While conceding this point, some might still argue that early childhood sins can't affect us because God doesn't punish us for unintentional sin. True, He does not. In the Law of Moses, although sacrifice had to be made for unintentional sin, no penalty was ever prescribed. And as Paul said, "In the past *God overlooked such ignorance*, but now he commands all people everywhere to repent" (Acts 17:30, NIV, emphasis added).

However, we still reap what we sow (Gal. 6:7–8), and that is different from direct punishment. If we take a walk on a moonless night and wander off a cliff, is God punishing us? Of course not. But did it make any difference that we didn't know the cliff was there in the dark? Did it make any difference that we didn't jump off intentionally? Of course not; we simply reaped the effects of the law of gravity. God's spiritual laws are no different. What we sow, we reap. When we sin, whether we do it intentionally or out of ignorance, the effects come back upon us. It's just the way life works.

So just how early can children sin? Psalm 51:5 says, "Surely I was sinful at birth, sinful from the time my mother conceived me" (NIV). There are those who admit that this verse teaches we are conceived in a sinful *state*. But they disagree that an unborn child can commit *specific acts* of sin, for no specific acts are mentioned in that verse. And they point out that Psalm 58:3 says we can sin specifically ("speak lies") *from* the womb (that is, *from* the moment of birth), but not *in* the womb.

To us, this sounds like an odd sort of hairsplitting. For if birth is the arbitrary cutoff point, what if a child is born three months premature? Does that make him able to commit a specific sin three months earlier than other newborns? Surely it must be Adamic sin, not the act of birth, that opens the door to such defilement, for God created birth to be clean and wholesome. Yet to satisfy those who raise this objection, here are scriptures

15

that more clearly reveal that we can commit specific acts of sin *in* the womb.

When Jacob's mother, Rebekah, asked God why Jacob and Esau jostled each other in her womb, God answered, "Two nations are in your womb; and two peoples shall be separated from your body; and one people shall be stronger than the other; and the older shall serve the younger" (Gen. 25:23). Verse 26 says Jacob came out of the womb grasping his brother's heel. His parents interpreted this to mean that he wanted to usurp his brother's place as firstborn, so they named him Jacob, "grasps the heel," which figuratively means "usurper." Jacob committed the sinful act of usurpation while still *in* the womb. *In* the womb, he jostled his brother. "*In* [not *from*] the womb he took his brother by the heel" (Hosea 12:3).

That pattern of usurpation continued throughout much of Jacob's life. He persuaded Esau to sell him his birthright for a bowl of lentil soup (Gen. 25:29–33). He dressed up as his brother and fooled his half-blind father, Isaac, into giving him Esau's blessing (Gen. 27:6–29). All this confirms not only that children can sin in the womb, but also that their sin can continue as a pattern into adulthood and even into the lives of their descendants. What began in Rebekah's womb is still going on today in the Middle East!

But even if they admit that unborn children are capable of sinning, some might ask, "Aren't our childhood sins under the blood?" Yes, they are. But if we are still practicing a sin, we have not yet yielded it to the cross. Some might ask, "Aren't we new creatures in Christ?" Yes, we are: "Therefore if any man is in Christ, he is a new creature; the old things have passed away;

behold, new things have come. Now all these things are from God, who reconciled us to Himself through Christ, and gave us the ministry of reconciliation" (2 Cor. 5:17–18). But this passage goes on to say, "...we beg you on behalf of Christ, *be reconciled to God*" (v. 20, emphasis added).

We have known many people who, according to family members, have come out of the womb angry at life and have continued that way into adulthood. When they became Christians, Christ reconciled them to Himself. But a Christian lifestyle requires that they respond by reconciling their angry hearts to Him, calling to death present patterns of anger that started so long ago, and taking up their crosses daily (Luke 9:23).

This is not about confessing childhood sins. Sins we ceased to practice before our moment of conversion were yielded to the cross when we prayed the sinner's prayer. No, it is about confessing ongoing adult sins that started in childhood. We go to the past to deal with the present. For instance, imagine that just a week before you became a Christian, your own mother tried to kill you, and you responded with deep resentment. Suppose the resentment continued beyond your conversion until the present day. Would you now say, "I don't have to forgive my mother or repent of my resentment; that is under the blood"? Of course not. You would forgive her and repent. Now imagine that she tried to kill you by trying to abort you when you were in the womb. If you are still resentful today, you must forgive your mother and repent of your resentment, no matter how early it started. For although God has reconciled Himself to you, your present resentment reveals that you have not yet reconciled yourself to God. That is why we go to the past—not to redo (and thus deny) what Christ has already accomplished, but to enable us to more fully respond to His already accomplished sacrifice. *in the way we live our lives now.*

So if this is really about present sins, isn't it enough to repent for present patterns and leave it at that? Can't we do that without revisiting events that happened long ago? Perhaps so, in many cases. But again, if your mother tried to kill you a week before you accepted Christ, wouldn't it help for you to talk out your feelings with God? Wouldn't you need His comfort to help you forgive? Or would you just tell yourself to "buck up" and "forgive" instantly? God does not require this. He not only let the psalmists share their hurts with Him, but He also gave them words to express them! And wouldn't you need to understand what it is that you are forgiving? Wouldn't it help to understand why your mother would do such a thing? How it affected your heart? What lies you were tempted to believe about yourself as a result? What lies you were tempted to believe about your mother and perhaps about other women? All this would deepen and enrich both your forgiveness toward your mother and your repentance of continuing resentment? *forgiveness toward myself for living my life as I have.*

Now back up a little. People whose mothers have tried to abort them or who were deeply hurt in other ways before birth often walk through life never having articulated such feelings and questions, especially since they cannot remember when and where their resentment began. Many have felt relieved to find out, through the witness of relatives and others, what happened so long ago and to finally find insights and words with which to process what they had always felt but could never articulate.

They also find it relieving to find that there was a reason why they have always had such deeply ingrained sin patterns. For instance, here is a composite story of many we have ministered to:

For as long as he could remember, a certain man had always felt irrational, violent rage toward any woman who rejected him, even if that "rejection" amounted to nothing more than her having to cancel a date because relatives came to visit unexpectedly. He felt ashamed for having no reason for such extreme overreactions. He always felt that there was something defective about him, but he could never put his finger on it. "Why am I different from other people?" he often asked himself.

When he found out that his mother had tried to abort him, he finally knew in his heart that he wasn't inherently defective after all. There had been a logical reason for the rages all along. That is, from the womb he had believed the lie that no woman (one) would ever want him. He was now able to articulate the pain he had formerly converted into rage. He was able to release the tears he could never release or even access. He went and talked it out with his mother, who admitted what she had done. Together, through hugs and tears, they were able to tear down walls between them that he alone had not been able to understand, much less tear down. In the process of getting in touch with the pain from his mother's violent intentions, he was enabled to empathize with the pain his rage had inflicted on the women in his life. And that enabled him to more fully own up to the sins he had committed against them and offer truer apologies. He forgave his mother, and they reconciled. He never again felt that rage. At the same time, learning how early his resentments had begun deepened his understanding of his own fallenness, and thus his need for Christ's saving grace.

Surely God has healed many without looking at the past. He is not bound to any one method. We should follow the Holy Spirit's leading and only focus on prenatal events as often and for as long as He deems that doing so is helpful. But when the Holy Spirit has led us to minister in this way, lifelong harmful ways of seeing God, others, and self have fallen from people's eyes like scales, in miraculous ways.

In our ministry we have observed that as a child grows, he will—unless the transforming power of the Lord intervenes—tend to interpret each succeeding experience in the light of what he has already perceived life to be and according to the way he feels about himself. His woundedness has clouded and colored his spiritual eyes. Dr. Verny's report says that a friendly or hostile womb creates personality and character predispositions and anticipation of the outside world. The Bible says in Matthew 6:22–23, "The lamp of the body is the eye; if therefore your eye is clear, your whole body will be full of light. But if your eye is bad, your whole body will be full of darkness. If therefore the light that is in you is darkness, how great is the darkness!"

Parents may give lavish affection to their child, and if it is received, it may be that their love may cover "a multitude of sins" (1 Pet. 4:8). But to reach the root level of a person's innermost being requires *light* in the person of Jesus Christ to penetrate the darkness in the heart of the one who is deeply wounded and confused; *truth* in the person of Jesus to counteract the lies the child has accepted about himself; the *forgiveness* of Jesus to cleanse, heal, and enable forgiveness in the heart of the child; and the *power* of Jesus to completely transform and make new.

Our mandate to invite Jesus to minister specifically to the deep levels of the heart so that truly the "inside of the cup" is cleansed is found in the following:

> Why do you look at the speck that is in your brother's eye, but do not notice the log that is in your own eye?... First take the log out of your own eye, and then you will see clearly to take out the speck that is in your brother's eye.
>
> —LUKE 6:41–42
> *Matt 7:3-4*

It may be that what we think we see as reality is not objective reality at all, but only our projection of the way we have learned to view life from our very beginning. We can have no new perspectives until we have been set free from the first binding influences of our early perceptions, which set the mold that shapes everything that pours into us. How often we read in the Scriptures, "Having eyes do you not see..." Daily we fail to see and understand one another and suffer hurt and pain and inflict the same. For instance:

A man works long hours because he loves his family and wants to provide well for them. His wife, out of resentment toward her father, who gave her no emotional support by his presence either before or after her birth, perceives her husband's absence as a sure indication that he does not care, that he does not love her, and that he is not a giving person. He, on the other hand, is bewildered by her hurt and anger and feels that he is in a "can't-win" situation with her. After a time, he may fulfill the image she has projected of him by succumbing to an extramarital relationship in which he feels more appreciated.

A young man suffered the devastation of being given away soon after his birth by his mother, who had conceived him illegitimately. A part of his response was to form a judgment deep

21

inside his heart that women will inevitably seek extramarital relationships and are not to be trusted. Therefore he "sees" every friendly gesture his wife makes among acquaintances as flirtation and projects his fear of being rejected again as false accusation against his wife. She loves him dearly, and it is strongly built into her to be faithful to him, yet she has to fight to keep from being driven by his insecurity into a position of vulnerability.

I (Paula) struggled for many years with the reaction of people I loved to what they described as my defensiveness. From my own point of view I felt that I was not being defensive. I was only "explaining myself," responding righteously to what seemed to be misunderstanding or unfair criticism and demand. It was difficult for me to receive helpful suggestions because to me they appeared not helpful but threatening. They seemed to insinuate that I had not tried hard enough or that I had failed to perform and was therefore not acceptable. Since I had already striven to do my best, my immediate compulsive response would often be to point out that fact to whatever primary person seemed not to be aware of it.

My response was, in effect, a counterattack and hurtful to others. As the Holy Spirit (and loved ones in the family) made me aware (with some difficulty) that I was often defensive entirely without cause, and that their love and acceptance of me was truly unconditional, I accepted the new "glasses" by faith and began to discipline myself to catch my reactions. But my eyes did not "see" with new vision until specific insight and prayer enabled me to do so.

It was difficult to recognize my problem as having originated in my family, for I was raised in a Christian environment where love was expressed genuinely and consistently, though not perfectly. Loyalty to and appreciation of my family hampered the search. Recognition of my negative reactions to criticisms and legalisms, which were indeed present in my upbringing, and prayers to forgive and be forgiven alleviated the intensity of my defensiveness but did not change the base of my reactions.

One day as John and I were returning from a speaking engagement (the theme had been unity), our own unity was severely fractured when it appeared that John was not at all able to understand or accept an important point that I was attempting to make in conversation. (At the time, he *had* to understand in the way I wanted him to, and I can't even remember now what it was that we were talking about!) I pressed hard to break through what seemed to be a stubborn and obtuse stance. I recognized the impasse as he sank into a deep cave and icicles covered the entrance. "All right, I give it to You, Lord," I said nobly to myself.

In the next moment I was overwhelmed by feelings I could not understand—the urge to throw open the car door and jump out! I was appalled. I had ministered to people who had done that sort of thing for one reason or another, but that was not the sort of thing I would do. I sat on it, and we continued home.

The Lord hears and answers the desire of our hearts. A short time later my mother came to visit. In the midst of conversation about many other unrelated things, she suddenly began to share with me about the experience of my birth. Soon after she and my father were married, her appendix burst. Peritonitis set in. With no modern miracle drugs to treat the infection, she nearly died. In those days (I am into the second half-century of my life) surgery was not accomplished by neat buttonhole incisions; she was opened from one side to the other.

After quite a long stay in the hospital, she was released with strong admonitions not to become pregnant for at least one year, preferably two. Within a few months, however, I was on the way. The doctor wrapped her abdomen in tight binders, and she wore those wrappings for support throughout her pregnancy, apparently with some fear that the growing pressure of me inside was a threat to her newly healed incision. There was certainly a threat to her health and, in addition, the constant fear of losing the baby. I came into the world crying, and only my father's presence (he was a traveling salesman) could console me.

As my mother related this story, the perplexing memory of my experience in the car came flooding with clarity into my mind. There was a meaningful parallel. In my mother's womb I was in a tight place, and there was a real possibility of a spontaneous abortion. Under the circumstances, my parents' response to my mother's pregnancy had to be ambivalent at best. In the car I was in a tight place and felt I was not being wholly received. I had the urge to abort the situation. We prayed about my birth experience as soon as I could share it with John, and I felt tremendous release and peace.

Some bonus benefits resulted: For the first time in my life I could begin to feel comfortable swimming. When on an airplane, I no longer felt compelled to balance it by leaning to the opposite side should it bank steeply. And I did not fight feelings of suffocation anymore when a blanket was pulled over my head or when I was kissed for a long time. All of these had related to feelings I had experienced in the prenatal state.

Later, prayers for my prenatal trauma revealed that I had felt guilty for being in the womb. This resulted in my trying to perform to earn a right to be and in my taking responsibility emotionally for endangering my mother. Consequently, I developed an overgrown sense of a need to control, to keep situations in manageable order. The sort of shyness with which I had struggled all of my life was identified by the one who prayed with me as being rooted in feelings deep inside me that if I grew, my growth would threaten another. This translated into feelings that if I grew in maturation, my growth would endanger John. And so I would hang back in fear and with hidden (to me) anger. This hampered John's and my working together. We prayed for all my in utero feelings to be healed. The prayers had a profound effect upon my life. My base of emotion has been drastically changed, and my perceptions have been significantly corrected. I am free to be me, knowing that my growth will not harm anyone and will only be a blessing.

Matthew 5:29 says, "And if your right eye makes you stumble, tear it out, and throw it from you; for it is better for you that one of the parts of your body perish, than for your whole body to be thrown into hell." We do not need to live in the hell of confused relationships. Jesus is available to do away with our old way of seeing through forgiveness and healing and to give us new sight by His Holy Spirit.

Luke 6 follows the call to take the log out of our eye with another figure of speech that indicates how we shall know if we have something in us that needs changing. Verse 43 says, "For there is no good tree which produces bad fruit; nor, on the other hand, a bad tree which produces good fruit." Common sense tells us that industrious taking away of bad fruit does not produce a healthy tree. We must deal with the roots of our tree.

Luke 6:45 follows in the same vein, telling us to look deep for the source of our problems: "The good man out of the good treasure of his heart brings forth what is good; and the evil man out of the evil treasure brings forth what is evil; for his mouth speaks from that which fills his heart." We begin to store treasure in our heart from the moment we become a living being; our treasure is made up of every experience we have ever had, the responses we have made to them, and the attitudes, judgments, and expectations we hold. Some, when evil comes out of the mouth, would like to say the devil made them do it. Be assured that if he did, he had to have raw material to work with. We cannot escape responsibility for what we do with our own treasure.

Jesus, in this Luke 6 sermon, is building to the punch line. Notice particularly that He is speaking to Christians, those who already call Him "Lord."

> And why do you call Me, "Lord, Lord," and do not do what I say? Everyone who comes to Me, and hears My words, and acts upon them, I will show you whom he is like: He is like a man building a house, who dug deep and laid a foundation upon the rock; and when a flood arose, the torrent burst against that house and could not shake it, because it had been well built. But the one who has heard, and has not acted accordingly, is like a man who built a house...without any foundation; and the torrent burst against it and immediately it collapsed, and the ruin of that house was great.
>
> —LUKE 6:46–49

The first six years of our life are our foundational years. By the time we are six, the structure of our character is formed. By the time we are ten, that structure is set in concrete. That is why there is deep necessity for death and resurrection when we come to Jesus. That is why we must be born again.

There is not one of us whose life was formed wholly on rock-solid foundations of perfect parenting. Besides which, most of us had some sinful reactions to the good parenting we did receive. Fractures in our early foundations, caused either by wounding inflicted upon us or by our sinful responses to events in our lives (or how we perceived those events), have weakened our ability to stand in time of trial or in the face of crisis. Then when the rains of daily pressures beat heavily upon us and the floodwaters of our anxieties rise, our stability crumbles.

When we are born anew in Jesus, we are in position to begin again, to have our foundations built again upon the Rock who is Jesus. As His Holy Spirit searches the innermost parts of our heart, we can repent of the treasured garbage that has been stuffed into our fractures and receive His foundation stones of a renewed heart, mind, and spirit. When we are born anew, we are born into the family of God, where we can receive human warmth and love to nurture our growth in a way our natural parents were not able to do.

If we follow our Lord's mandate to dig deep and lay our foundation upon the rock, we will have no cause to fear anything that comes into our lives. Unfortunately, much of the Church has thought that process to be some sort of suddenly-arrived-at-magic when we accept Jesus as Savior. Many have failed to recognize that being born again means that one is a baby, merely ready to begin the process of growing up. These have failed to press on to take hold of that inheritance for which Christ Jesus has taken hold of them (Phil. 3:12).

Often, responsibilities that can be handled only by the mature in Christ are given to the newly born. Thus they are thrust into positions of leadership before their fractured foundations have been discovered and repaired. Vulnerable, they fall, and in that fallen state often suffer the condemnation of fellow Christians who do not understand. The foundational call of Luke 6 cannot be avoided without great damage and loss. Neither can Colossians 3 nor Ephesians 4. The laying aside of the habits and practices of the old self (that are developments on the foundations of our early years) and the putting on of the new (which is made possible because of what Christ has accomplished for us) is clearly a process following the truth that "you have died and your life is hidden with Christ in God" (Col. 3:3). *Warning:* People who set out to "dig deep" in the power of their own flesh rather than by the guidance of the Holy Spirit accompanied by the balancing nurture of the body of Christ can very easily become merely navel-gazers, reinforcers of self-centeredness.

In the process of serving, laying down our life for others, the Holy Spirit will uncover in us those areas of persistent problems for which we need some deep searching and healing. We can then confess our faults to one another and pray for one another that we may be healed (James 5:16). We do not have to be stuck with the mess inside us. No matter what our stage of life, Jesus is able to reach to the little child within to enable forgiveness, administer healing to our deepest wounds, and effect change.

Clues for Identification of in Utero Wounds

The Condition in Utero	Commonly Observed Patterns of Attitude and Behavior after Birth
A child is not wanted.	Striving, performance orientation, trying to earn the right to be, inordinate desire to please (or the opposite, rejecting before he can be rejected), tension, apologizing, anger, death wish, frequent illness, problems with bonding, refusing affection (or having an insatiable desire for the same)
A child is conceived out of wedlock.	Having a deep sense of shame, lack of belonging
Parents face a bad time financially.	Believing "I'm a burden."
Parents are too young, not ready.	Believing "I'm an intrusion."
Mother has poor health.	Guilt for being; child may take emotional responsibility for mother.
A child being formed is what one or both parents consider to be the wrong sex.	Sexual identification problems, sometimes one of the causes of homosexuality, striving to please and to be what the parents want, futility, having a defeatist attitude, "I was wrong from the beginning."
This child follows other conceptions that were lost through death.	Being overly serious, overachieving, striving, trying to make up for the loss, anger at being a "replacement," not getting to "be me"

Clues for Identification of in Utero Wounds

The Condition in Utero	Commonly Observed Patterns of Attitude and Behavior after Birth
Mother has inordinate fear of delivery.	Fear, insecurity, fear of childbirth, fear of death
There is fighting in the home.	Nervousness, uptightness, fear, jumpiness, jumping in to control a discussion when differences of opinion emerge, feeling guilty ("I'm the reason for the quarrel"), parental inversion (taking emotional responsibility for the parents)
Father dies or leaves.	Guilt, self-blame, anger, bitter-root expectation to be abandoned, inordinate hunger to find the love of a father figure, having a death wish, depression, homosexual behavior caused by hunger for a father's love
Mother loses a loved one and is consumed with grief.	Deep sadness, depression, death wish, fear of death, loneliness, imagining, "No support for me; I will have to depend on myself."
There are unwholesome sexual relations; the father's approaches to the mother are insensitive or violent, or there is more than one sexual partner.	Aversion to sex, fear of male organ, generally unhealthy sexual attitude
Mother is afraid of gaining too much weight, does not eat properly	Insatiable hunger, anger, guilt about being a burden

These observations are those we have discovered during many years of prayer ministry. Many are very much the same as reported in Dr. Verny's research. He added several more, among which are:

The Condition in Utero	Commonly Observed Patterns of Attitude and Behavior after Birth
Mother is a heavy smoker.	Predisposition to severe anxiety
Mother consumes much caffeine.	Baby likely to have poor muscle tone and low activity level
Mother consumes alcohol.	More than the chemical effect, the baby absorbs the negative feelings that caused the mother to drink.
Breech delivery	Higher risk of having learning problems
Unusually painful delivery	Anger, lacking acceptable outlet, having ulcers, depression
Relatively normal delivery	Fury if pain (mother's or child's), seems to confirm rejection or ambivalence in utero
Induced labor	Can affect mother-child bonding, can contribute to masochistic personality or sexual perversion
C-section	Inordinate craving for all kinds of physical contact, trouble with concept of space, clumsiness
Cord around neck	Throat-related problems, swallowing, speech impediments, can contribute to antisocial or criminal behavior

For those who would like to delve further into the treasure of research that has been done on this subject, Dr. Verny included an extensive resource list in the back of *The Secret Life of the Unborn Child.*

But let us share more of our own personal experiences. These cannot be observed under a microscope, weighed, or measured, but they happened to us; the Lord gave us insight, we prayed accordingly, and the prayers bore good fruit.

John and I were sharing about the healing of the wounded spirit at a seminar for prayer ministers. Loren, our oldest son, was also one of the speakers. As we taught about prenatal and birth traumas, Loren was hit with the answer to a question he had been puzzling about during all of his adult years. Why had he always, against common sense and training, so fervently resisted going to bed at a decent hour? Why, when his wife retired at ten, did he feel a compulsion to busy himself with one thing after another until the wee hours of the morning when finally he was so tired he *had* to go to sleep?

He and Beth have a very good relationship. He loves to snuggle. He wanted, for health's sake as well as for effective ministry, to obtain sufficient rest. He recognized the pattern as one he had expressed all his life. As a baby he would keep some part of his anatomy moving as long as he possibly could in order to stay awake, no matter how exhausted he became. As a toddler he would persistently drop again and again over the side of his bed and run about the moment the lights were out, despite all that we could do to persuade him otherwise, and so on. As I finished speaking, Loren shared the new insight the Lord had given him: "I have to stay awake because if I go to sleep, I could die."

How had he come to think this way? This is what we discovered. John and I were married while we were still students at

Drury University in Springfield, Missouri. Loren came on the scene immediately, and John still had three years of graduate school ahead of him. We spent the summer after graduation in St. Louis with my family before we went on to Chicago Theological Seminary a few weeks after Loren was born. I was nineteen; John, twenty-one. We had no money with which to pay medical bills and seminary tuition except what we could earn day by day, but we were determined. Idealistic determination does not produce the same sort of peace and rest that real faith and trust provide, and at that point in our lives, I'm sure we had more of the former.

I was at a church picnic playing baseball when I went into labor, and it was not until the next morning that I knew what was happening. No one was allowed in the labor room with me. I remember fighting fear and loneliness and praying, "God, don't let me die!" then feeling foolish that I should even think such thoughts because, "I am a strong person," I told myself. The doctor, without consulting my family or me, gave me a strong dose of ether, unaware that warnings had been given years before that I should never be given it. When I first saw Loren, he was pale blue and extremely sleepy, and he remained that way long enough to cause everyone some concern. We had to work hard to keep him sufficiently awake to eat. Research had not yet revealed that alcohol, drugs, and anesthetics given to mothers are immediately experienced by the child in the womb. No wonder his little spirit was afraid to sleep. He had received the message, "I have to stay awake because if I go to sleep, I could die."

When Loren finished sharing this and more about how it related to his compulsive workaholic tendencies, everyone at the seminar gathered around him and prayed for him to be set free. And he was.

Our daughter Ami demonstrated the truth of the observation of some medical researchers that ambivalence in the parents can result in lethargy in their child. We were in seminary, not wanting another child at that time. But here she came; we were certainly ambivalent—we do love her, but right then when money was tight and energies so low? Ami began life as a tubal pregnancy. I spent ten days in South Chicago Community Hospital with my feet elevated. Prayer, a small miracle (the Lord moved her), and good medical care worked together to save that precious life. But when Ami was born, she was so sleepy she would hardly eat. Throughout her early youth she seemed to be sleepily dreaming through life, unable to take hold. Further prayer for healing of her wounded spirit called her forth to blossom and take hold of her life dynamically. Prayer also set her free from fear of tight places.

Mark was the next to be conceived while we were still in seminary, and we had to fight to prevent a repeated threat of miscarriage. We certainly did not want a third child right then. He also had to be called forth by prayer to take hold of his life. And the Lord showed us that the dyslexia he struggled with in his early years was a physical manifestation of his spirit fleeing from life. Feeling unwanted—a third child when two were a financial strain—he did not want to be born. His feelings of expecting to be rejected caused subsequent scramblings of other parts of his being. The healing of his spirit and the disciplines he himself exercised to walk in his healing have now become part of the strength of his ministry as a gifted prayer minister, and today Mark is completely healed of dyslexia.

Many references have been made by researchers to images they believe have registered in the memory streams of children in utero, which then float to consciousness sometime later, usually in response to similar experiences that trigger recall. It is difficult to prove the validity of such information, but the testimonies are so common that they must be given serious consideration.

One such story was told to us by our son John, and we still chuckle when we think of it. The triggering mechanism (at least that which caused him to share) was the difficulty we were having with this very strong son's struggle during his teenage years to become an individual. He related to us what was sometimes his dream, sometimes a daydream. He was in a dark, cozy place, and someone wanted him to leave, but he liked it in there and didn't want to go. He was happily occupied, playing with a long rope that he would handle, stretch it as far as it would come out, wrap it around himself, bat it, and shake it. The game gave him great pleasure. He was angry to think that he had to leave this place.

John was rather embarrassed to share this, but he was serious in wanting to identify some meaning in such a persistent picture. I was excited as I then shared with him that I had carried him nearly six weeks past the due date, that when he was born it was by induced labor, and that the immediate response of the nurse in the delivery room was one of intense concern. John's umbilical cord was extremely long. It was wrapped several times around his neck, and the little fellow was all tangled up in the rest of it. We laughed together through my apology. We prayed. We wonder what would have happened had we allowed that little person (who has always responded, "I want to do it myself") to do it himself by sending the message, "I'm ready to be born," which we now know every unborn child normally sends to trigger the birth process.

Researchers now know that a baby chooses his own time to be born. He sends a message to his mother's body to start the labor process. If a child does not get to choose his time, then he may have residual angers all of his life. John had inexplicable angers. A softball game probably induced labor for Loren three weeks early. Loren always had an irrational hatred of the game of baseball, until the Lord healed him.

John was one of our planned babies. He did not exhibit the list of behaviors that Dr. Verny associated with induced labors, but perhaps some of those virulent angers originated there. We had to think we might have wounded him by our impatience to get him here. On the other hand, thank God for His redemptive power and for His healing, which not only creates glory from the death of our mistakes but also enables us to laugh at ourselves as well.

My husband, John, and I have sometimes joked about our call to minister to the Christian family and how that necessitated our raising six children because we are such slow learners. We don't really believe that; each of our six was a special gift from God. But it is true that wisdom accumulated as we all loved one another and matured together as a family. Tim and Andrea, coming last, did not have to suffer as much from our ignorance as did the older children. But God has provided the same for all—healing the wounded spirit and wholeness as His redemption reaches every depth and area of our lives. We knew that we had to pray for healing for Tim and Andrea as soon as they were born. They probably have been the most secure and relaxed of our half dozen. But

God also has provided for them the spiritual exercise they need to make them strong, and He will continue to do so through their and all our lives. The fact that all of us have been wounded so as to need healing is not necessarily a negative. Our Lord would build joyful, grateful, victorious hearts; tenderness; compassion; sensitivity; and wisdom out of our healed hurts.

Whether you are praying for a baby or an adult, the reality of Jesus affecting the spirit of a person is made possible through prayer for the innermost being of the tiny child inside the one for whom you pray. Jesus Christ is not confined to our dimension of time and space. He can identify with and heal our spirits at any time—past, present, or future. Our entire life is an open book to Him. Therefore, it is a simple matter for Him when we pray, asking Him to identify with a wounded spirit all the way back to the time of conception. When we have asked Jesus to make this identification, we speak the comfort, reassurance, and affirmation of the Lord directly to the spirit of the child. We pray something like this:

> We say to you in the name of the Lord Jesus Christ that your life is not a mistake. God made you in the love that He is. He called you into being at the right time and right place. He prepared a way for you and gave His life for you. You are a privilege, not a burden; a joy and a delight, not a disappointment. You are not an intrusion; you belong. You are a treasure just because you are, not merely for what you can do. You are one of Father God's own children, and He delights in you, and we delight in you.

We go on to ask the Lord to destroy whatever lies the child may have accepted and to bring to the cross every resultant destructive attitude, expectation, and personality structure or habit pattern. We pray with vivid imagery, seeing the Lord pouring His love all about the child and inviting him to grow into the fullness of his own life, restfully, as God planned for him from the beginning. We pray that the child be enabled to forgive those who wounded him. We also pray that the child himself be forgiven his negative responses. We pour the healing love of Jesus into the wounded spirit like a healing balm. We ask the Lord to give the person a sovereign gift of trust, rest, and peace and to cause his entire being to be integrated with wholeness and harmony as he is reconciled to being who he is where he is.

Then we place the cross of Christ (the stopping place for all sins) between the child and his parents and his parents' parents, all the way back through his generations, declaring that all of his inheritance be filtered through that cross. This is not magic. It is simply a way of putting the Lord in charge and of claiming His blessing and protection. (Every person must make that claim for himself at some time during his life, as he becomes ready.) All descendancy of evil and every curse coming to the child through his family must stop on that cross. We ask the Lord to hide the child in His own heart and to cast light into the eyes of any powers of darkness who might attempt to oppress, afflict, or prevent his life. We stand in the Lord's authority against such powers.

Finally, we place a blessing in the name of Jesus on the person's life. We ask the Lord to melt any hardness of heart, to strengthen with might in the inner man (by which we mean his spirit), to enlighten the eyes of the heart, to open doors for him, to draw him to his destiny, and to place a mantle of protection on him for all his future life.

Concerning Prayers Using Imagery

We do not ask the person for whom we pray to form a picture in his mind that is in any way contrary to the way an experience actually occurred. We do not ask the inner man to accept a lie. Lies never effect healing, nor do they lead to freedoms that can last. We do ask the person to forgive everyone who was involved in each hurtful experience as he remembers it. We encourage him to ask forgiveness for his own responses. We assure him of that forgiveness, and we break the power of the habit patterns that resulted from his cherished and practiced responses.

For us, praying with vivid images means that we describe clearly and colorfully *the picture the Lord gives us* to convey new life to the person once the old has been done away with by repentance and forgiveness. We do not make up a picture by our own flesh, nor do we ask the person to take some kind of soulish trip in his imagination. All such things are neither necessary nor very helpful. We ask the Lord to give us a word picture or a visual picture or symbol that will minister appropriately to the need of the individual, and we then describe it as accurately as we can. The person receiving ministry may be the one who receives the picture from the Lord, or he may receive a portion to add to that which we are describing.

CONCERNING EMOTIONAL RESPONSES TO PRAYER

We welcome the expression of emotions, but we do not pressure anyone to get in touch with them. Emotions can be deceptive. People are capable of creating emotions to please the person who is ministering to them, to dramatically attract sympathy, to satisfy the belief that valid experiences are always accompanied by tears, or simply to express something that is more of a religious cultural habit than it is an individual's specific expression of repentance or release. Such ways of creating emotions may be totally unconscious. Tears may even be a diversionary tactic to cover up what is really going on inside. They may also come as a real outpouring to which wrong labels can then be attached.

We say that if emotions come up naturally and easily as a result of prayers, let them flow freely. But let us not strive to make them happen. It may be good if we do experience some emotional releases at the time, but we should not judge the efficacy of prayers by the presence or absence of emotions. It may be that months later emotions will come to the surface as the Lord brings something to ripeness. When that happens, the healthy response is to let oneself feel, and then hand those feelings gratefully to the Lord as the One who has drawn them up from the depths of the heart. It is well to remember that much healing is realized, without any emotions, simply as the fruit called "changed behavior."

It is easy to pray for spiritual healing for a tiny baby newly arrived in your family. As you hold the baby to feed him or rock him, feed him with love and prayer again and again. Close friends of ours made it their ministry for years to take foster babies into their home. Most of these little ones were rigid, fearful, restless, and colicky when they first arrived. But after much hugging, rocking, sweet talk, and prayer of the sort that we have described, such babies would relax and respond beautifully with alertness in joy and go into adoptive homes ready to melt into the new parents. Our friend, as the temporary foster mother, would talk to each tiniest baby about the joy prepared for him in his new home and how Jesus would be going with him. Our friends adopted one such child themselves whom the doctors had feared would be mentally retarded because of neglect, abuse, and malnutrition. The love and prayer combination effected a miracle in that little boy, and today he is an adult who is bright and healthy and secure in love.

Children under ten or so may be tucked into bed at night with prayers of thanksgiving for them and for the blessing that they are. Such prayers should be repeated over and over, until the children receive in the depths of their spirit that they are cherished. Very young children may be prayed for aloud as they sleep, and their spirits will hear the prayer and be gradually secured in love. Older children who manifest a wounded spirit can be sensitively drawn into conversation about their fears and animosities, and the source of these can be explained to them in simple terms. They can then be invited to participate in prayer either actively or by consent and asked to voice their forgiveness and to choose life.

Beyond prayer, persist with affection. Give them the material things they need, but far more importantly, give them *you*. Play games. Do things together as a family. Laugh. Joke, but do not tease; little children do not understand teasing at all. Don't be threatened by their questions concerning natural parents (if they have been adopted). Do not conceal the fact of adoption. In their spirit they already know, and if you do not make that known consciously, they will feel betrayed or lied to. Guide them to a compassionate understanding of why they were given away and to express forgiveness. If you are talking with your own natural child about early woundings for which you feel responsible, do not be afraid to ask his forgiveness.

Do not be overly anxious to straighten out your child merely to appease your own conscience. He will naturally be healed to a large extent as you allow the Lord to deal with your own inner man. Address the child's problems by conversation and prayer only when they persistently corrupt his attitudes and actions. Let your discipline be firm, loving, consistent, and appropriate to the trespass and the child's maturity level. Compliment. Affirm. Let your love be unconditional. Give your child opportunity to express his feelings. Give him room to fail, and let him have the assurance that he will never lose your love. Know that you are in the resurrection business to bring him to fullness of life, but don't wear that responsibility too heavily. God is in charge.

You *will* make mistakes, but God is bigger than your propensity to fail. You may have to repeat prayers and verbal affirmations many times. This does not indicate lack of faith or mean that the first prayers and affirmations were ineffective. It simply demonstrates the fact that when a little child hears the good news that he is loved, he says, if not with his mouth, certainly with his heart, *"Tell me again!"* until that message permeates the very fiber of his being.

When we pray for the wounded spirit of an adult, we do not pray without his consent for specific changes in his spirit. It is an invasion of privacy to mess around with the insides of another who must stand in relation to the Lord and be held accountable for the condition of his spiritual life. (There is one exception. Where husband and wife are concerned, they may pray more specifically for one another because they are in a one-flesh relationship. However, the Lord neither smiles upon nor honors manipulation, and each partner is held accountable for insensitivity to the other.)

We believe that general prayer for the Lord's love and light to shine on another is always in order, for that creates an environment in which the person is enabled to come to freedom to make good choices. In Ephesians 1:18–19 we are given a good prayer example that is appropriate to anyone: "I pray that the eyes of your heart may be enlightened, so that you may know what is the hope of His calling, what are the riches of the glory of His inheritance in the saints, and what is the surpassing greatness of His power toward us who believe." In Ephesians 3:16 we find another: "...that He would grant you, according to the riches of His glory, to be strengthened with power through His Spirit in the *inner man*..." (emphasis added).

The goal of healing the wounded spirit is that all might be able to say to God, as we read in Psalm 139:

> For Thou didst form my inward parts; Thou didst weave me in my mother's womb. I will give thanks to Thee, for I am fearfully and wonderfully made; Wonderful are Thy works, and my soul knows it very well. My frame was not hidden from Thee, when I was made in secret, and skillfully wrought in the depths of the earth. Thine eyes have seen my unformed substance; and in Thy book they were all written, The days that were ordained for me, when as yet there was not one of them....Search me, O God, and know my heart; try me and know my anxious thoughts; and see if there be any hurtful way in me, and lead me in the everlasting way.
>
> —PSALM 139:13–16, 23–24

CHAPTER 2

OVERCOMING WOUNDS FROM PRENATAL REJECTION AND BIRTHING TRAUMAS

> Behold, children are a gift of the Lord; the fruit of the womb is a reward. Like arrows in the hand of a warrior, so are the children of one's youth. How blessed is the man whose quiver is full of them.
>
> —PSALM 127:3–5

Our son Loren, who was also our pastor at the time, asked in church one Sunday how many knew that they were unwanted children when they were first conceived. More than half answered in the affirmative. He then asked how many just a few months or even weeks later were very much loved and wanted. Almost all of that same group raised their hands. Then he made a statement in rebuttal to the cry "every child a wanted child" by those

45

who support abortion on demand: "I hardly think that parental rejection early in pregnancy is an indication that the poor infant will lead a miserable life after birth."

I thought of my own inopportune birth and of the fact that four of our six children were uninvited blessings. Memories of wonderfully warm and happy childhood experiences flooded into my mind: laughter at family gatherings, weekend excursions in the car, wild scooter rides down our alley, romps in piles of crispy autumn leaves, delightfully ooey-gooey mud puddles, trips to the St. Louis Zoo, my brothers imitating the monkeys for a week afterward, the smell of clean sheets, carefully prepared meals we shared together, the Sunday morning hassle of getting us all to church, roller-skating on the black satin of our asphalt street…

Through it all ran deep assurance of our belonging, even while we were being spanked for our transgressions. "This hurts me more than it hurts you" may have brought forth an "Oh, yeah?" response from our heads, but our hearts knew they really did hurt for us too. Love was real. Our own children can describe the same as their inheritance.

Most of the woundings we received in our spirits early in life have been, and continue to be, healed in the laying down of life for one another and by the presence of the Lord in the process. Specific woundings, set into the patterns of our lives by our sinful responses, have been and are being dealt with as the Holy Spirit reveals them to us. "Surely our griefs He Himself bore, and our sorrows He carried" (Isa. 53:4). For that reason we are more and more enabled to appreciate and celebrate the joys of being who we are. As I witnessed those raised hands in the church service, I was also aware of the great number in Cornerstone Fellowship who had received prayer for the healing and transformation of their inner man from us, from the pastor and elders, and from the people in their home fellowship groups.

God intends that all of His children be received as blessings and rewards. A "full quiver" does not means doing without the good things of life, but realization of the fullness of life, if priorities and perspectives are in line with the mind and heart of God. What society in general has not yet discovered is that there is a God who will comfort all our waste places and make our wilderness like Eden and our deserts like the garden of the Lord (Isa. 51:3). Unfortunately, the body of Christ has not fully discovered that in real terms either.

During the time we attended Cornerstone Fellowship, there was a family there with seventeen children. Thirteen of them were adopted. Most of those thirteen were racial minorities and handicapped—some disabled physically and some mentally. The world says that it would have been better if none of those children had been allowed to live. Yet each one of them has been healed, blessed, and set free by consistent, lavish, physical affection and heartfelt, spirit-penetrating prayer. Everyone in Cornerstone would have felt sadly diminished had we not had the opportunity to minister to them and they to us. We were painfully aware that each of those precious children was, by the circumstances of conception, a prime candidate for abortion, according to the view of a large portion of our society.

The following quote is a reprint of an editorial from *California Medicine*:

> The traditional Western ethic has always placed great emphasis on the intrinsic worth and equal value of every human life regardless of its stages or condition. This ethic has had the blessing of the Judeo-Christian heritage and has been the basis for most

of our laws and much of our social policy. The reverence for each and every human life has also been a keystone of Western medicine.... The process of eroding the old ethic and substitution of the new has already begun. It may be seen most clearly in changing attitudes toward human abortion. In defiance of the long held Western ethic of intrinsic and equal value for every human life regardless of its stage, condition, or status, abortion is becoming accepted by society as moral, right, and even necessary. *It is worth noting that this shift in public attitude has affected the churches, the laws, and public policy rather than the reverse.* Since the old ethic has not yet been fully displaced it has been necessary to separate the idea of abortion from the idea of killing, which continues to be socially abhorrent. The result has been a curious avoidance of scientific fact, which everyone really knows, that human life begins at conception and is continuous whether intra- or extra-uterine until death. The very considerable semantic gymnastics which are required to rationalize abortion as anything but taking a human life would be ludicrous if they were not often put forth under socially impeccable auspices. It is suggested that this schizophrenic sort of subterfuge is necessary because while a new ethic is being accepted the old one has not yet been rejected.[1]

I share the following story in the hope that it might make the body of Christ more fully aware of the healing power through our Lord Jesus Christ to redeem, transform, and bring to glory the "impossible" lives the new ethic would have eliminated.

REJECTION BY ABANDONMENT

Benny was born three months prematurely, weighing in at only a couple pounds. His parents already had young children and were not at all prepared to accept the responsibility of a growing family.

The neighbors were accustomed to hearing the baby cry, but one Saturday night they called the police when the crying went on until after midnight. Benny's parents had left him in the care of the other children while they went to the bar to drink. Benny, who had been clad only in a very soggy and smelly diaper, was wrapped in a blanket and taken to a shelter home. It was quickly apparent that there was something seriously wrong with him. The medical examination discovered several life-threatening maladies, and Benny was immediately hospitalized. Once he reached an acceptable weight in the hospital, he was released into the custody of foster parents.

Benny had not been secure in the womb of his natural mother, nor had he been welcome in her arms. But he certainly found warmth and love in the embrace of his foster mother, who with her husband and children began a rebirthing process in him the moment he arrived in their home. His new foster mother literally carried him night and day. His little body had become stiff. He could be balanced like a board on the palm of a hand. He was listless and glassy-eyed and unresponsive at first to anything around him. The doctor feared that he would be brain-damaged because of poor nutrition.

His foster mother spent hours massaging his little body. She rocked and cuddled him, carried him on one arm as she did her housework, sang to him, talked to him, and nearly wore out his neck kissing him; at night he slept on her chest. She daily poured the Lord's healing into him by prayer. Prayers were not only for the strengthening of his physical body, but also much more for the healing of his wounded spirit and for calling him forth to life.

It was not long before the baby began to respond with alertness to his nurturing environment. His new family was delighted with him, as was his church family. Every Sunday after worship admiring friends gathered around him at coffee hour to celebrate his progress. It became more and more clear that he was so integral a part of the family that they couldn't let him go. Neither his natural parents nor his grandparents contested his adoption that followed shortly afterward.

Benny suffered through many hospitalizations in his younger years, but the prayers continued. He was built up with vitamins and more holding and more prayer.

By the time Benny was in middle school, he was of normal size, and his development certainly indicated no brain damage. Later he became a vigorous and healthy teenager with normal teenage interests and problems. He was more able to give and receive affection than most of his peers and has a better-than-average willingness to explore in prayer ministry the hidden depths of his heart, which had held some self-destructive attitudes and anger.

The miracle of love is that Benny is a survivor of circumstances that would have killed another child. The wonder of his rebirth is that he has the capacity to trust, to hold his heart open, and to press on. The areas of conflict with authority figures he encountered as a teenager have not broken the bonding he has with his adoptive parents, particularly with his mother, as so often happens even with nonadoptive parents and teenagers. Watching so closely the process of healing in Benny's life confirmed to us once again the truth that love does indeed overcome a multitude of sins (1 Pet. 4:8). "He heals the brokenhearted, and binds up their wounds" (Ps. 147:3).

In Benny's case, the past that needed healing and transforming concerned little more than the prenatal and birth traumas. That being the most powerfully influential period of anyone's life because it is the seed out of which the rest of life grows, persistence in ministry was necessary to overcome the fruit of intense rejection and neglect. But that persistence was exercised step by step *during* the laying of each building block of his foundational years. That foundation, which was in itself healing despite imperfections, will continue to be made new as the Lord works in his life. *Phil 1:6* "I am confident of this very thing, that He who began a good work in you will perfect it until the day of Christ Jesus" (Phil. 1:6).

We have stated that Jesus is able to transcend time and identify with us at *any* stage of our development to set us free from those dated emotions and expectations that shape the basic structure of our being and hold us in bondage. Let us now consider another case, one that began with much less wounding initially but compounded day by day for thirty-five years before Jesus was given access to heal.

Rejection by Parental Emotional Withdrawal

A man came to us in a state of emotional and physical exhaustion. He was functioning in his job by sheer determination but was suffering from chest pains, anxiety attacks, nausea, and sleepiness so overpowering that, while driving, he would frequently have to pull off the road to nap. He was plagued with persistent feelings that he would die young and fears that his wife would die too. No matter how much he slept, there was never enough rest for him.

In the previous ten years he had held ten jobs. He had been subject to frequent illness all of his life; he was still a prime target for every cold germ or flu virus that came along, and an ulcer gave him considerable discomfort. Finances were in poor condition, his present boss was always pressuring him, and his father was dying. No matter how diligently he applied his skill at work, projects seemed to collapse. At night he put off going to bed, not wanting to let go of the day; in the morning it was overwhelming for him to face the day. Sometimes he would become so stressed he would throw up. He existed in loneliness, even in the middle of a crowd, bemoaning the lack of permanent relationships. "In my whole life everything has gone wrong." "Why can't I make anything work?" "What is missing in me?" "Why do I always turn out to be the victim of other people's decisions?"

As we explored this man's history and observed him closely in his relationships, we discovered that because he had never developed the power to be his own person, he was overly subject to the decisions and actions of others. The message "Tell me what to do" came from him unceasingly. His sense of worth and belonging was dependent on how well he succeeded in pleasing others. He worked so hard to please that others felt his striving and desperate need for appreciation as too heavy a burden. His unconscious demands for approval were a drain upon friendships.

We observed that his need to succeed, though it was often for the sake of others' welfare, was so intense that he would over-promote and overorganize, causing people to feel pushed and crowded or helplessly swept along with him. They would resist his efforts and eventually withdraw from him personally. He began to look upon money as his only real security and mark of worth.

He had not been an unwanted child. After unsuccessful attempts at childbirth, he was finally conceived. His mother exercised every possible care to protect her pregnancy, but she lived nine months in an attitude of tension and fear of losing another child and could not let her heart go in joy of anticipation. This was confusing to her, and she was often depressed. Those emotions and that reserve registered in the spirit of her unborn child.

> Recent research indicates that abortion results in depression during a subsequent pregnancy and immediately post partum. This depression from abortion or *loss of a previous child* appears to delay a mother's preparation for her newborn by diminishing her anticipation. It has long been recognized that a significant personal loss without completed grieving will interfere with subsequent attachments...seems to truncate the mother-infant bonding mechanism so that it does not develop as well in subsequent pregnancies.[2]

This man's mother had not completed the process of mourning the loss of her babies and was unable to bond well with him as a result. Neither was she ready to risk giving herself unreservedly. Her heart was still self-protectively insulated. Her new baby experienced that withdrawal as abandonment. Neither parent was demonstrably affectionate, though they provided well for him materially. A small child understands and accepts love in terms of touch, not intellectual reasoning, so this circumstance continued to affect him adversely.

When the man was a young boy, his older brother died. Since the man had never felt completely accepted and had entertained some jealousies in relation to his brother, he assumed guilt for that death. As his parents sank into grieving for the lost boy, the man's guilt was confirmed to him. He responded by becoming convinced that he had to strive to accomplish enough to make up for the others. Somehow he had always felt like a replacement from the beginning, and now he had to live for the brother whom the parents had so dearly loved. Of course that was not what the parents wanted. But in his perception he was in a no-win position. He had to fill the vacancy in order to earn a place for himself. But by doing so, he could never *be himself.* He could never even admit his anger, because anger did not elicit pleasant responses from those he tried so hard to please.

> Behold, Thou dost desire truth in the innermost being, and in the hidden part Thou wilt make me know wisdom.
>
> —PSALM 51:6

The man's healing was accomplished over a long period of time. First, in conversation we drew him out as much as we could to intellectually understand the dynamics working in his life as we have just described them. He declared that he wanted to be whole. We asked him to consciously reject the lies he had accepted from the beginning about his own lack of worth and belonging. In prayer we asked the Lord to minister to his spirit deep inside. Until then, the grown man remained trapped in the emotions he had experienced at the beginning of his life.

We called those lies and the power of those emotions to death in the name of Jesus, and we spoke directly to his inner being (as in the prayer we described in chapter 1) to direct and enable him to take hold of his new identity: "I am a child of God. I am chosen. I am precious. The Lord loves me because I am." We said to him, "If you do everything right, you won't be loved any more than you are now. If you do everything wrong, you won't be loved any less. You *are* loved; you didn't earn it, and you can't lose it. It is God's gift to you. Before your parents knew you were on the way, God had created pathways for you to walk in. No one can live your life in the same way that you can. God has preserved your life for you, and He wants you to walk restfully in it. You were not created to be a replacement for anyone else."

> Before I formed you in the womb, I knew you…
>
> —JEREMIAH 1:5

> For we are His workmanship, created in Christ Jesus for good works, which God prepared beforehand, that we should walk in them.
>
> —EPHESIANS 2:10

We poured the balm of the Lord's healing into him and asked the Father to hold him until he was enabled to come to rest in the heart of the Father. We asked the Lord to write the truth of his belonging on his heart. Then we asked him to forgive his parents. We did not get involved in trying to determine their actual guilt. We were dealing with his perceptions, his subjective reality. In such instances, forgiving others does not say that others are actually guilty. It says that we are guilty of unforgiveness. This kind of forgiveness is a matter of recognizing that we have made a sinful judgment against others for what we believe they have done, and now we are releasing them from our condemnation and are choosing to bless them instead.

Then we went on to the more important aspect, his need to be forgiven himself for all the responses he had made to whatever his parents did and for his responsibility for the life he had built on that base by his conscious and unconscious choices. We "saw" the Lord coming with His sword of truth to cut him free from the past, real or imagined, and to lead him forth into the fullness of his own destiny and purpose. We loosed him to be himself, to grow up inside himself in the power of the risen Lord. We prayed that the Lord would continually strengthen him in his spirit as he walked in the new way.

The man needed specific absolution for the guilt he felt for his brother's death. We did not try to reason with him about false guilt; we knew that he needed more than comfort. He was guilty of jealousy and of wishing he could have his brother's place. Therefore he needed forgiveness for the murder he knew was in his heart, even though he had never experienced it as a conscious fantasy. He felt guilty. Saying something reasonable, like, "All little brothers are apt to feel jealousy and sometimes wish a brother would die or go away," only gives such guilt a place to retire for a time. Feelings of guilt are done away with only by assurance of forgiveness through the blood of the Lord Jesus Christ.

Prayers of affirmation and assurance were repeated each time he sank back into old familiar patterns. We prayed again and again that performance orientation would come to complete death. Beyond that, it had to be written on his heart that he was worthy of being chosen and that others would take the initiative for him even when he didn't deserve it. We hugged him a lot. We visited. We ate together.

I remember one evening when he pulled one of his periodic pouts and retired to the bedroom to wallow in the self-pity of "nobody cares about the hopeless case that I am." We followed him there to declare that we knew what he was doing, that there was no way he could cause us to be so frustrated with his repeated flopping and imperfectly disguised manipulating that we would drop him. "We are your family. That is a forever relationship. You can't lose us." Finally after much perseverance he came to rest with us, with God, and with himself. A number of years and many miles separate us now, but there is warmth in the memory of rebirthing one who will forever be a cherished part of us.

The important point to note here is that this man's wounding started in the womb. He was, in a sense, a replacement. His mother's unhealed grief had left a void to be filled, rather than that he could come to fulfill a joyful expectation. If he had been fully received and nurtured with physical affection, as Benny was, much of his wounding would have been healed in the course of his growing up. But as it was, the lack of real nurture from his mother and father compounded his woundedness. This man's case is typical of many.

REJECTION BY UNSUCCESSFUL ABORTION

Far more wounded are those whose parents tried to abort them and failed. Their lives are usually plagued with frequent illness. They tend to struggle with periods of depression. Some attempt suicide. They have initially received the message, "You *should* die." Unconsciously they are keyed to respond to that. Some women try to abort their babies because someone tried to abort them. The golden rule works in their lives inside out and upside down. If they judge others, they *will* do to others what has been done to them, until the saving power of the Lord intervenes.

Observations we have made in prayer ministry were confirmed by a statement in *The Zero People*:

> Our clinical observations tend to confirm the reports of others; even young children know of their mother's early pregnancy, abortion, and miscarriage.[3]

The book reports the case of a five-year-old who became severely disturbed by his knowledge that his mother had aborted a child when he was only two and a half. A seven-year-old reported a dream in which three siblings went to play with him in a sand bank. It collapsed and the three were buried. He didn't know them, but somehow he was sure they were brothers and sisters. His mother admitted to having had three miscarriages but insisted there was no way he could have known.

Our purpose for this book is not to explain absolutely how such knowledge is possible, except to say that the spirit of a tiny child is extremely sensitive and his intellect as yet uncluttered. He seems to be able to tune in with keen receptors to things we adults might miss.

Studies show, and our experience confirms, that children who "know" in their spirits that brothers or sisters have been lost by abortion or miscarriage often experience a gnawing sense of guilt, as if it were somehow their fault. Such children may harbor an emotional distrust of parents for fear of what might be in store for them.

Parents who have aborted a child because they were unable to provide financially, because it was inconvenient to have a child, or because of social pressures will no doubt struggle to make sure they don't find themselves in that predicament again. The uptightness of these parents will reflect in the attitude and behavior of children already born into the family. Such children may interpret the fact of their survival in the family as a result of their being desirable only at that particular time. They may feel pushed to perform to maintain that desirability. Their sense of belonging becomes conditional. When disharmony rises in the family, they may express extreme anxiety and possibly assume guilt for the presence of the quarreling.

A child whose sense of conditional belonging has been reinforced many times by family tensions may actually feel guilty for existing, helpless to do anything about it. He may react in his feelings of unworthiness by neglecting himself or trying to commit suicide. Or he may go to the other extreme and break out in anger that says in effect, "I didn't ask to be born. But here I am. I'm going to demand my place, and I'll prove to everybody that I have the right to be a person!"

We have ministered to some who unconsciously but vigorously styled their lives to punish their parents. "I'll show you! I'll throw away my glory, and you'll never feel any pride on account of me. You didn't want me, and you deserve to be ashamed." In those cases, of course, the self-destruct message is operating as well as vengeful rebellion that desires to inflict pain for pain. Our prescription is always the same: healing of the wounded spirit by prayer, confession, repentance, forgiveness, and establishment of a new identity in the Lord Jesus Christ, followed by continuing human nurture through friendship and affection.

Such a person may need to be carried a long time in the heart, which means that a rebirthing and spiritual parenting process may have to follow if healing is to be maintained. The spiritual parenting relationship is temporary, but it must continue so long as the Lord indicates necessity. We must not pray and then drop such a person and run. That will likely only reinforce the problem; he always "knew" he was supposed to be aborted. Or, he "knew" it would happen to him as it had to his lost siblings who were not pleasing to his parents.

AFFECTS OF ABORTION ON THE WOMAN

In the world today, approximately 46 million abortions are performed per year. Per day that amounts to 125,000 abortions! Seventy-eight percent of all abortions are obtained in developing countries, and 22 percent occur in developed countries. About 26 million legal abortions are obtained each year, while an additional 20 million abortions are obtained in countries where it is rejected or prohibited by law. The worldwide, lifetime average is one abortion per woman! In the United States, the number of abortions was 1.37 million in 1996. That's 3,700 per day. Women twenty-five years of age and younger account for 52 percent of these abortions. Women between the ages of twenty and twenty-four obtain 32 percent of all abortions, teens 20 percent, and girls under the age of fifteen 1.2 percent.[4]

To us who daily repair the damage done to women who have swallowed the lie that their baby is only an object they have a right to discharge, this series of statistics is excruciatingly painful, to say nothing of God's precious children whose lives have been taken from them. What grief to our loving Creator in whom every life is so precious. He died for each and every one! The body of Christ must learn to forget its differences and war in unity for the sake of women and their unborn children! Pray that this awful carnage be stopped.

Publicity for and against abortion is before us constantly. Every high school or junior high school girl knows that abortion is a legal option. It is common for people in our society to weigh the value of buying a new car and a bigger house against that of raising a child, and for the child to lose. Many abortions are performed because of the devaluation of children. It has been suggested by some that because of this general devaluation of children, coupled with the general breakdown of the stability of the nuclear family, children tend to devalue themselves. They have less and less confidence they will be cared for, and less and less hope for the future—thus the increase of depression in our young people and mounting statistics that already show suicide to be the third major cause of death in young people between the ages of fifteen and twenty-four![5]

We at Elijah House Ministries have ministered to literally hundreds of women who have come by the Holy Spirit's gracious ministry to realize that they have murdered their children. Some never find their way to us or other ministries. Suicide is often the result, and suicide is not the only resultant death factor.

One study, based on the information obtained from the death records of 173,000 low-income female residents of California who received Medi-Cal state health care coverage, says:

> Women who have abortions are at significantly higher risk of near and long term death than women who give birth...almost twice as likely to die in the following two years [after an abortion]...[and have] a 154 percent higher risk of death from suicide, an 82 percent higher risk of death from accidents, and a 44 percent higher risk of death from natural causes.[6]

A government-funded study conducted in Finland in 1997 revealed that:

> In the first year following an abortion, aborting women were 252 percent more likely to die compared to women who delivered and 76 percent more likely to die compared to women who had not been pregnant. Many of the extra deaths were due to suicide.[7]

Though these studies say nothing further about causes, those of us who minister so often in this field cannot help but speculate that the higher incidence of deaths following abortions may in large part be caused by the fact that the sin of abortion fractures the shield of defense God has placed over all of His children. "The wages of sin is death" is far more practical and real than many who give lip service to God's laws would like to admit. It is not that God wants death to happen. Rather, the reverse. But His laws cannot be mocked. Abortion is a seed sown to death (Gal. 6:7), and death is reaped—unless something allows God's grace to intervene. We just cannot flaunt God's laws with impunity. Death stalks those who sow it.

REJECTION BY PARENTS' PREOCCUPATION TO PROVIDE

There are many other ways we inflict deep spiritual wounding on our children by devaluing their worth. Wounding can occur in families who have remained together but are so concerned with providing a living that measures up to their desired material standard that they fail to nurture the children for whose sake, they protest, they are working.

Recently I interviewed the principal of a day-care center. She was concerned for a preschooler who seemed listless, withdrawn, disinterested, and unable to participate with other children. The child was the only son of a corporate executive whose wife was also rising in a successful business career. The mother was called in for consultation. "Our child is the most important *thing* in our lives" actually meant that they were careful to give every *thing* they could think of to their offspring. But the only regular time spent with him was a forty-minute ride through heavy traffic on the way to school each morning and thirty minutes spent religiously between the supper hour and bedtime reading a story to the little fellow.

He occupied an inviolate place in a busy schedule, just like all the other people who waited for their appointments. But the only real affection he received came from a nanny who brought him home in the late afternoon, fed him his supper, and came in to tuck him in and turn the lights out after the parents had retired to their guests or other pursuits.

Most working parents are not so blind as that, but scores of thousands of lonely children live in pockets of isolation from their parents, not really knowing what it is for which they yearn so sadly. They don't understand the sources of their sudden upsurges of anger, often when daddy has just run in to present them with a delightful new toy on his way to a golf game. "See you later," he says, and goes away. Or when mother, hurrying to put supper on the table, says, "Don't bother me now! We'll talk about that later." She has come home from work late, exhausted, and feels the pressure of an evening too short to accomplish her chores. But to her child who needs to share, "later" sounds like "never" and probably is.

Even though children may accept with their minds that all of the busywork is for their well-being and that it means they are being cared for, they starve inside for loving attention and physical affection; they interpret the whole of life in an attitude of futility. The more material goods they are given, the more they demand because *things* have become a substitute for love. Things are not love; they don't satisfy—thus the need for more and more. Disappointment builds anger. Anger at parents is then projected onto all authority figures and God. Respect for property disintegrates because material wealth has come out the winner in the competition to be the parents' "dearest treasure." Vandalism is sometimes a means of trying to "kill the enemy." Some children steal because they have been stolen from.

Let us say clearly that it is not the fact that both parents work that causes a child to be wounded. Motivations, attitudes, and priorities make all the difference. Sometimes both parents must work to pay rent and provide bare necessities. In one such family we see both parents sharing household chores and involving their children without laying too much responsibility on them. They all work together, and they play together. Family TV, games, fishing, camping, and popcorn making are corporate enjoyments. And they pray together. Money always seems to be scarce, but its presence or absence does not seem to affect the basic foundations of love.

Foundations of love may be fractured in children whose mothers returned to work too soon after they were born. Babysitters, be they sweet grandmothers or PhDs in child psychology, are still only substitutes for the real thing, and babies know it. God has designed babies to need their mothers and fathers to enfold them in physical embrace so that their spirits flow together to accomplish bonding between them. Breast-feeding is far better than bottle-feeding. Holding and rocking are essential. The *active* presence of the father in the day-to-day care of babies is necessary to provide strength and structure as a vehicle for tenderness. A baby comes to rest as he puts down spiritual, emotional, and mental roots in the consistent, reliable nurture of parents who are always there when needed. Trust is built into his nature at root level. Most birth traumas can be healed in those early months.

If a baby is left occasionally with a babysitter, basic security need not be shaken. Rather, it could have the same effect the "peekaboo" game teaches: "Now you see me. Now I'm gone. Here I am again, and it's all right." But when a small baby is left all day, day after day, with a sitter, he feels abandoned by the parents no matter how physically well cared for. Seeds of confusion are planted about identity, belonging, and worth. Full bonding does not develop between the child and his parents. In fact, if a child learns to accept and look for nurture from a very loving babysitter who cares for him all day, and if the child spends only a short time each day with his parents, he may at first be torn between the two and then choose to bond with the one who has invested more vitally in his care. Being taken from that environment can cause as grievous a wound as the death of a parent.

We have ministered to countless numbers of people who in their adult years felt an unusually deep warmth and gratitude for grandparents who essentially raised them. "I was close to them, but I could never really talk to my parents." In such cases there is always a need to heal the wounded spirit. Such people live with unanswered, nagging questions: "Why did my parents not put me first?" "Why didn't they love me more than what they were doing?" "Was there something wrong with me that they didn't want to be with me?"

When such children become adults, they rationalize and excuse their parents, but rational understanding of circumstances does not yet accomplish healing in the heart. Only the Lord Jesus can enable forgiveness and reach through time to set an individual <u>free from foundational insecurities so that he can restfully, trustfully expect to be chosen, cherished, loved, and nurtured today by those who are primary to him.</u>

SIGNS OF CHILDHOOD REJECTION

How do we know whether ministry for early registration of rejection is still required or if love from someone has already overcome a multitude of sins? Simply by evidence of fruit in the person's life (Luke 6:43). Consider these questions:

- ◈ Are the person's feelings easily hurt?

- ◈ Does he perceive hurt where none was intended? Does he nurse hurt feelings?

- ◈ Does he take personally, as insult or slight, remarks that others would ignore, laugh at, or enjoy?

- ◈ Is he habitually defensive of himself and others?

- ◈ Does he have to have a special invitation or encouragement to participate in activities others would simply volunteer to join?

- ◈ Does he demand attention rather than invite it?

- ◈ Does he withdraw into himself and find it difficult to share?

- ◈ Does he talk a lot without revealing what he really thinks?

- Does he need compliments but fail to hear them?

- Does he expect to be overlooked?

- Does he neglect his appearance or anxiously spend too much time or energy on it?

- Is he prone to jealousy in relationships?

- Does he put himself down (or brag too much)?

- Does he have trouble following through with projects he starts?

- Does he always seem to be a spectator on the outside looking in?

Unhealed rejection is often projected onto others. Ben's father left before his son was born. His mother hated this man, who had first abused and then abandoned her. Since Ben was very much like his father in appearance and temperament, she unconsciously projected her feelings toward her husband onto her son. As he matured, the relationship became more and more hurtful.

Ben was, of course, deeply wounded, and in no way was it built into him to expect anything but rejection. He drew it to himself from friends, from his wife, and even from his own children. He managed to get himself fired from job after job. Often he would anticipate being fired and quit his job before his boss could move to dismiss him. As Ben began to receive ministry and prayer for inner healing, he was compelled to test again and again the sincerity of those who ministered to him.

Bringing the negative to death on the cross is a relatively easy task. Common sense and the Holy Spirit's gift of discernment discover problem areas and root causes. Applied prayer is effective because of what Jesus Christ has already accomplished on the cross. His resurrection power is also available, but learning to walk in that power is a process.

> As you therefore have received Christ Jesus the Lord, *so walk in Him*, having been firmly rooted and *now being built up in Him and established in your faith*, just as you were instructed, and overflowing with gratitude.
> —Colossians 2:6–7, emphasis added

> He has now reconciled you in His fleshly body through death, in order to present you before Him holy and blameless and beyond reproach—*if indeed you continue in the faith firmly established and steadfast*, and not moved away from the hope of the gospel that you have heard.
> —Colossians 1:22–23, emphasis added

Those who minister to individuals with the kinds of stories we've told in this chapter must build them up and help them become established in their faith so that they may walk in Him rather than in what all their previous life has trained into them. They may often find themselves saying, as Paul did in Galatians 4:19, "My children, with whom I am *again in labor until Christ is formed in you*..." (emphasis added).

It may seem like a never-ending pregnancy till Christ is formed in some with whom we are in labor. Daniel was abandoned by his mother and father when he was five. His grandmother chose to care for his sisters but wanted nothing to do with the difficult job of raising a boy, so he was placed in a foster home. As wounds of rejection erupted into displays of anger and rebellious behavior, Daniel was moved to another home, and then another, until he arrived at the eighth. There the foster parents said, "Look, we know what you're doing. You are testing to see if we'll kick you out. We won't, so you may as well settle down and decide to be a part of our family."

When Daniel was eleven, he was adopted by his foster family and continued to respond positively in many areas to their love. But some patterns persisted for a long time: difficulty in applying himself consistently in school, choosing friends who were ne'er-do-wells, skipping school with them so frequently that he lost credits. His choice to wear ragged jeans and tattered T-shirts communicated his lack of self-esteem much more than it reflected a teenage fad. And in his later teens, what we called "the foster child syndrome" persisted.

He would disappear for a week at a time, spending a day or two at one friend's house until he had worn out his welcome, then going to another friend's home to do the same thing. When friends or his own energies were exhausted, he would return home to shower and sleep long hours, only to repeat the behavior. His response to frustrated job hunting was, "Nobody wants me." His choices did not begin to change until people who loved him persisted in expressing that love unconditionally along with discipline that delivered the message: "God and we love you just as you are, but we love you too much to leave you that way." Continuing prayer began to give him the strength to see where he was trapped and to make some positive choices to break out of built-in patterns and take hold of his life. Continued healing of his wounded spirit still empowers those new choices today.

John and I often teach concerning what we call "see-through faith," which those who minister effectively must have. This is the kind of faith that looks beyond present circumstance to celebrate what the Lord is accomplishing by the struggle we are presently, totally, and perhaps frustratingly involved in. "See-through faith" is "the assurance of things hoped for, the conviction of things not seen" (Heb. 11:1). It is made of the kind of love that "bears all things, believes all things, hopes all things, endures all things" (1 Cor. 13:7) for the sake of the one who cannot yet do that for himself. While we are yet "in labor" until Christ is formed in those whom we carry in our hearts, we will hurt with them and for them, even as Christ does. But in that identification is joy, as we read in John 16:21: "Whenever a woman is in travail she has sorrows, because her hour has come; but when she gives birth to the child, she remembers the anguish no more, for *joy* that a child has been born into the world" (emphasis added).

CHAPTER 3

CUDDLE TIME

For this reason, I bow my knees before the Father, from whom every family in heaven and on earth derives its name, that He would grant you, according to the riches of His glory, to be strengthened with power through His Spirit in the inner man; so that Christ may dwell in your hearts through faith; and that you, being rooted and grounded in love, may be able to comprehend with all the saints what is the breadth and length and height and depth, and to know the love of Christ which surpasses knowledge, that you may be filled up to all the fulness of God.

—EPHESIANS 3:14–19

aby cries. Somehow mother recognizes in the cry the sound of hunger. She lifts him from the crib, and the child responds excitedly—reaching, breathing quickly, at once laughing and crying, nestling into oneness with the warmth of her, patting, pinching, pulling, drawing from the free-flowing fountain—milk leaking out the corners of his mouth, squeaking, gulping—round tummy, fat cheeks, feet that seem to pump to make more room, soon heavy eyelids, satisfaction, falling limply to sleep again—tiny lips that nurse in sweet dreams of more and more...

Any mother who has loved her child as she nursed him at her breast knows that the babe was drinking far more than milk. There was a meeting taking place in which she knew the sometimes breathtaking joy of her baby's new spirit flowing into hers, seeking, asking. And her own spirit, full to bursting with sweetness, rose to embrace and pour into that little one with power she couldn't begin to understand. She knows that there has been a sharing of life and love beyond description, a sharing that has fed and fulfilled them both.

That quality of nurture can never come in a bottle. It has always been the Lord's best design to feed each infant with his mother's own liquid-love-with-skin-on-it. Man will never improve on that plan, though certainly the Lord is capable of blessing all necessary substitutes.

Our purpose here is neither to quicken feelings of guilt nor to arouse the pain of loss in any mother who out of misinformation or incapability did not nurse her baby. It is solely to make the reader aware that there may reside in an adult unidentified senses of hunger, insecurity, rejection, anger, frustration, disappointment, or emptiness traceable to very early experiences at, or away from, the breast of the mother.

Perhaps a mother attempted to nurse and her milk was lacking nutrients. Though her child was fed, he was not satisfied. That continually repeated disappointment can register in the foundation stones of his being and create an expectancy to ask but not to receive richly and abundantly. It can dwell in him as a vague and mystifying fear and inability to rest in and trust another's love or ministry. It can contribute to an inner drive to search or strive beyond necessity. Such a person may later be blessed beyond measure in many ways, yet never seem (at the deep feeling level) to have enough.

A baby may be thriving on mother's milk, but circumstances may interrupt: Mother becomes suddenly ill. Baby's teeth appear early. He bites and will not be taught not to. An infection develops in the nipple. For whatever reason, the baby is suddenly deprived. In his spirit, he may resent the substitute. He may feel at levels below reason a sense of rejection, of losing what is rightfully his. He has no well-developed intellectual faculty with which to put his feelings into proper boxes. He simply reacts and lives with those seeds of "I've been robbed" and "I won't get mine." Later experiences in life may reinforce or trigger those deep feelings. As an adult he may find himself responding in relationships in seemingly unexplainable, childish, self-centered behavior. Sometimes we have found the loss of breastfeeding to be the reason some people cannot stop smoking; the oral sensation, the comfort and peace of smoking reach too deeply into unsatisfied areas.

The good news of our Christian faith is that when we become aware that we have such reactions, we have only to confess by faith that we do own hidden resentments and avail ourselves of the blessedness of giving and receiving forgiveness. We may invite the Lord Jesus to meet us at that deep level of our being, and in the person of His Holy Spirit, He will comfort and satisfy our spirit deep within. He will then release us from bondage to childish structures, and we will find that we more and more easily catch ourselves in what have now become recognizable habit patterns over which we now have some authority. In the process the Lord will graciously give a gift of growing trust, which will open the heart to receive more readily the warmth of human affection from friends, who will then be enabled to help us to come more and more to life.

Quite often we have ministered to married couples who were unable to talk out their differences because when irritation arose or the threat of quarrels appeared, one (or both) experienced instant fear that sent them fleeing either into isolation or into frantic attempts to explain, settle, or smooth over. Or they were simply overwhelmed by emotion, paralyzed in any capacity to act in relation to the other: "I feel trapped. I want to get out, but I can't!" They may have been convinced they wanted out of the marriage altogether, that the only thing holding them was the children, responsibility to God, lack of enough money to live separately, the fear of what people might think, and so on.

The truth of the matter may have been that deep within there was a seed of anxiety that was planted firmly when they were in the crib and parents were quarreling loudly in the room. They felt the tension, took into themselves the destructive energy of the anger, and reacted in panic as they felt the protective strength of mother-father love cracking and splitting. The sky was falling! The world was coming apart! A mechanism of self-defense by fleeing or turning off was born. Now when they are grown, any argument releases the explosive power of the baby's terror, magnified by years of reinforcement each time the family atmosphere became tense or a position was threatened or the clamor of voices was heard. For such people, the Lord is close at hand to identify the seeds of fear, sort them out, and bring them all to the cross.

* Identify the seeds of fear
- Sort them out
- bring them to the cross

HEALING FOR CUDDLE TIME TRAUMAS

When we minister to people who have suffered from emotional or physical interruptions during their earliest moments of being nurtured, we have them pray a prayer something like: "I see that I reacted in fear when I heard my parents shouting. I made a sinful reaction to that. I fled from life (or the opposite, I charged headlong in order to control). Forgive me, Lord. Enable me to forgive in the deepest levels of my heart. Set me free from consequent habit patterns. Fill me with Your love that is never threatened and never threatens. Establish me in You, root and ground my spirit in love, and protect my heart so that I may not need to react wrongly." It is not enough to pray that the grown one be set free; there would remain a memory, causing the person to continue to cringe in fear deep inside. It is the little one inside to whom we invite the Lord.

It is seldom as effective for a person to pray for himself as it is for another to pray for him. To choose to expose the fear inside ourselves and to open our heart to another person is an act of trust that denies the tyranny of our feelings. This act prepares in us the way of the Lord, which has always been to bring us to life by the loving nurture of family and friends. What was not done for us in the beginning can now be done for us in prayer by others who care. Expressions of care and prayer may need to be repeated again and again until our inner self catches on to respond in a new way.

Since the heart of a child naturally opens in trust to quiet, sensitive strength, the voice of the one who prays for the innermost being of another needs to communicate the tenderness, warmth, and enfolding love of the Father. The attitude of the

75

person praying needs to convey the unconditional love of God through Christ Jesus. The prayer minister should pray with an arm around the shoulder or invite the other to rest his head against him. Prayer for the inner man is most effective when vividly pictorial.

We have found this way of praying to be not at all dependent on our own insight but rather a gift of the Lord through committed and consecrated imagination. The Holy Spirit is quite capable of turning our perceptions of the person's confessions into a beautiful picture of healing that the Holy Spirit projects upon the screen of our minds as we pray aloud the new reality He wants to communicate.

We may find ourselves praying something like this:

I see, Lord, that there is a little one deep inside my friend who is afraid, lonely, hurting, and hungry. He needs to be held in arms that are secure and strong. Thank You, Father, that Your arms are like that, and that right now You are reaching deep down inside to enfold that baby with the warmth and strength of Your own being. I know that You, Father, are delighted with the little one whom You fashioned out of Your own heart of love. This one, Lord, is chosen and precious, a treasure to You. You are pouring Your sweet light into Your child until all hunger is satisfied, all anxiety is settled, all fears are calmed. Hold this one, Lord, until the love that You are permeates every cell of his being and enables him to melt into You, trusting. Thank You, Father, that You are light pushing back

darkness; You are music displacing noise; You are
a perfectly safe place to lie down to rest. You will
never leave, nor will Your love fail.

The Lord may inspire the prayer with pictures of rocking, walking the floor, comforting with hugs and pats, tucking into bed, standing watch—all the things a parent is called to do for a baby.

In the depths of a woman who finds it difficult to confidently express a need or her opinions to her husband or any man, there may be a tiny child whose cries in the night were answered by an angry face looming large over the rails of the crib and an angry voice booming its displeasure. At the root of overwhelming irrational feelings of loneliness may be many childhood experiences of being left alone for hours at a time to cry in a room behind closed doors. Beneath the apologetic attitude of a woman who cannot easily receive loving attention for fear of burdening others may still live the heart of a baby who remembers in her subconscious mind rude, rough, angry handling by a bothered parent, for instance, as her messy diapers were changed.

Recognizing foundational experiences behind the structures in our flesh and thus seeing the driving forces within us today is only the first step in the process of transformation. We must then assume responsibility for the choices we made, confess attitudes that sowed the original bramble seeds into our life, and lay the entire matter on the altar of God, submitting ourselves to Him without explanation or defense. The Lord will then accomplish that forgiveness in our hearts (Matt. 6:14). He will bring to death the old structures with their practices (Col. 3:3–9), comfort and strengthen us from inside (Eph. 3:16; 2 Cor. 1:3–4; Isa. 51:3), give us a new heart (Ezek. 11:19; 36:26; Jer. 24:7), and grow us up into new life (Gal. 2:20; Eph. 4:15; 1 Pet. 2:2–3).

We are not capable of changing our hearts by an act of our wills. But by the continual act of our wills to invite the Holy Spirit to do that work of transformation in us, and by the consistent quiet discipline of "reckoning as dead" (as Paul describes in Romans 6:11) those symptoms that may continue to persist for a season, we can contribute substantially to our process of coming alive—or we can by prideful stubbornness and lack of trust remain in our predicaments.

More difficult to deal with than the negative experiences of our infancy is the lack of those positive experiences that should have brought us to life. It is by warm, affectionate touching and holding that the spirit of a child is called forth to fullness. If a baby has not been held, cuddled, rocked, sung to, walked with, and talked to, but has been cared for only in terms of rigidly scheduled feeding and bedding, he will most likely become an adult who interprets all of life in like manner.

For example, he may be uncomfortable with spontaneity and unable to open wide the heart and nestle trustfully into another's love. His security and satisfaction may be in the smooth operation of schedule and plan, his definition of love in the giving of material gifts and services. But because his spirit knows there is something more to life, he will experience hunger he cannot identify. He may find anger welling up from inside that he tends to project onto those around him as though they should be providing some comfort for needs he cannot name. Family and friends may be offering that nurturing comfort consistently and abundantly, but he may fail to perceive and receive what is given.

He may still think he is being starved in the midst of a family banquet of offered love.

A person's soul (as we understand it) is that structure of character and personality in which his spirit resides. If that structure has been imperfectly formed by a lack of affectionate nurture and discipline early in life or if it is damaged by abuse, the spirit of the person may fail to develop or lack equipment to express itself healthily. In adult life he will then be crippled in his capacity to receive and contain spiritual nurture from friends and loved ones. Blessedness may be heaped upon him, but he will not be able to make it on his own. The answer for him is not to be found in exhortations to "count your blessings," not in "try harder" or "wake up." He has no tools in hand with which to do those things. He simply is incapable to do so no matter how hard he tries.

The answer lies in consistent repeated prayers for the spirit of the inner man to be held in our loving Father's arms, for the Spirit of the living God to flow into him with life-giving power to affirm, to quicken, to resurrect, to bring him into all the fullness of life in the Father (Eph. 3:19). The inner one is like a little child, and so he says, "Tell me again. Tell me again." He needs many repeated prayers. Christians who pray with him may need to associate on a regular basis as spiritual mothers and fathers in Christ to do for him what his natural parents failed to do.

Though we do not rely on techniques of role playing, psychodrama, and the like to minister to deep needs in people as much as we rely on the simple working of the Holy Spirit in the hearts of people following prayer, we do not at all discredit their use where the Lord directs. Many times we have seen tears streaming down the face of a person whose stance has been a long-practiced, cold, intellectual poise. The stimulus that unlocked the emotions was no more than a brush of hands on the shoulders and a hug here and there as he walked slowly between two rows of loving people as they sang "Cause Me to Come." What began as a drama to illustrate our flowing through the river of life banked by the supportive love of friends became an instrument by which God could penetrate into the depths of the heart. The mind, not expecting the exercise to amount to more than sentimental ritual, was off guard, and love scored a victory, penetrating defensive barriers.

We have witnessed strong men sobbing as they were rocked gently by groups of two or three. "Rock-a-my soul in the bosom of Abraham" was sung as a lullaby, and in the simplicity of the experience, love somehow pierced through strongholds of controlled emotions to hidden needs and melted the stony heart. In most instances, there arose a new ability to feel and to reach out, because the babe-like spirit inside the grown adult had received a portion of the ingredient of love so essential to life.

Such experiences, however, must be followed by ministry that supports, encourages, and protects, or else the newly born can become like the seed in the parable of the sower that dies by being choked among tares (Matt. 13:24–30). Without continuing ministry to enable him to become rooted and established in the Lord in his new capacity to experience life (which includes at the same time vulnerability to hurt as well as openness to blessing), he may feel abandoned, exposed, and fearful. If he flees back inside himself to the seeming safety of the old familiar prison, it may be a long time (if ever) before he allows himself to be put in a position where he might be awakened again.

It is often difficult for the person being ministered to, to accept that his present emotional responses are rooted in and fueled by experiences and reactions made in infancy. This is especially so if life has written on his conscious mind vivid recollections of bits of positive nurture.

A young man who was about twenty-two years old came to me (Paula), brokenhearted that his wife had left him and condemning himself because it was largely his uncontrolled temper that had driven her away. He could not understand the eruptive violence that caused him to hit her occasionally when pressed by argument. He was mystified by his fierce possessiveness and by the intensity of his fear that the relationship could not be mended. He was even more mystified by his inordinate feeling that he would not be able to live without her.

He had been raised by loving, attentive, affectionate grandparents who had brought him up in the church. They had disciplined and affirmed him well. There were other children in the home with whom he had enjoyed good fellowship. He had no recollection of having been abused, unduly criticized, deprived, or rejected. He was not aware of any partiality that had been shown to others or of having developed a competitive spirit. Family had always seemed to be there when he needed them. Everything he could consciously remember would seem to have equipped him well for participation in a comfortably happy marriage relationship; consequently, his behavior seemed a total contradiction.

"What happened to your natural parents?"

"I don't remember my mother at all. I think my parents were divorced soon after I was born. I don't know. My dad came around once in a while. But my grandparents were always mom and dad to me. I don't remember being an unhappy kid."

I explained that the spirit of a young child experiences far more than he can know with his mind and that it is possible that he had known in his spirit the absence of his parents and had felt hidden hatred for his mother leaving him altogether. Further, I asked him to consider whether an unconscious desire to punish his mother might cause him to project onto his wife the anger and fear belonging to his mother, causing him to hit his wife when in verbal battles she seemed to desert him emotionally. I asked if the possessiveness he felt toward his wife could not actually be an intense, unidentified reaching out to claim the mother he had never really had. I asked if the jealousy he directed at anyone who claimed his wife's attention might more properly be aimed at those faceless people and events that had taken away the mother he could not find even in his memories.

"Wow! That sounds far out! But I suppose it *could* be. I haven't found any other answer."

The young man consented to offer to God, in faith, what he could imagine might have been in the heart of a baby who felt abandoned by his father and mother through whom he had received life. *By faith* he repented of anger and resentment for being rejected, of all judgments he could have made toward his parents, particularly against his mother. *By faith* he repented of possible anger and mistrust of God for having allowed such a thing to happen. In all this he was not aware of any negative feelings in himself. "For I am conscious of nothing against myself, yet I am not by this acquitted; but the one who examines me is the Lord" (1 Cor. 4:4). "Who can discern his errors? Acquit me of hidden faults" (Ps. 19:12).

I (Paula) declared that if these possibilities were in fact true, then by the authority of the Word of God (1 John 1:9) he was forgiven the unconscious sin of dishonoring his parents. And together we invited the Lord to wash his heart clean all the way back through his years to the beginning, to comfort and strengthen the little one in his innermost being, and to fill him with the Lord's gift of forgiveness that could flow to those parents wherever they were. We prayed that the cross of Christ might in a real way come between him and all his past, that he might be free from inside to become the new creature the Lord called him to be.

He left our office, touched by the prayer, grateful for the session, but with the attitude, "OK—I'll wait to see if anything comes of this. Nothing else has worked."

Several weeks later the phone rang. Greeting me was a jubilant young man anxious to share the unbelievable.

> You'll never guess what happened! My real mother looked me up! Right out of the blue she called me! We met and had a wonderful visit!

He went on to share the pieces of the puzzle he had never been able to get hold of.

> My mother loved me! But my parents were *so* young. And they couldn't support a marriage. My grandparents had the marriage annulled just after I was born. And there was some kind of big court battle for custody of me, and my grandparents won. And my mother wasn't allowed to see me! She's been hurting and afraid all these years. Now I have to work at forgiving some other people, but my mother really loved me! Isn't that terrific? I don't know if my wife and I can get together again or not. But I feel different inside about it. I'm going to *live* no matter

what happens. I know I don't have to *force* her to do anything anymore.

The circumstances of that young man's life had not been changed by his trying harder to demonstrate Christian love or virtue or by his striving to be a loving husband. The important thing to note is that it was the bitter roots within him from childhood (his hidden, unconfessed sinful character structures) that had continued to produce bad fruit in his life despite his conscious efforts. Not until he confessed by faith that hidden area of sin did the Lord have invitation to transform that protected, unconverted depth of his heart.

In inner transformation we are always evangelizing, "converting" level after level of the heart in order to bring us wholly into line with what our conscious mind has committed to the Lord—all this to bring ultimately to an end that inner battle described by St. Paul in Romans 7:18–19, 21–24: "For I know that nothing good dwells in me, that is, in my flesh; for the wishing is present in me, but the doing of the good is not. For the good that I wish, I do not do; but I practice the very evil that I do not wish...I find then the principle that evil is present in me, the one who wishes to do good. For I joyfully concur with the law of God in the inner man, but I see a different law in the members of my body, waging war against the law of my mind, and making me a prisoner of the law of sin which is in my members. Wretched man that I am! Who will set me free from the body of this death?"

The "body of this death" does not mean the physical body but sinful character.

It has always amazed me (Paula) that we in the church family do what we would not think of doing in the natural family. Who of us would bring a baby home from the hospital, put him in a crib, toss him the car keys and a list of chores to do, and leave him with an ultimatum to do everything right or else? But that is exactly what we have done to countless newborn Christians. Because they have been "born again," we have heaped responsibilities upon them and have demanded instant performance according to standards in Christ that they are as yet in no way prepared to accomplish emotionally or experientially. And how quick we have been to judge their errors with condemnation!

Lest I fall into the trap of condemning those who condemn others, let me close this chapter by laying that judgment of mine (that the Church *should* know better) on the altar and go drink another glass of milk (1 Cor. 14:20).

CHAPTER 4

TODDLING TERRORS

When I was a child, I talked like a child, I thought like a child, I reasoned like a child. When I became a man, I put childish ways behind me.

—1 CORINTHIANS 13:11, NIV

From an adult perspective, toddlers are delightful mixtures of cuddly comic, lap wiggler, furniture climber, drape swinger, messer-upper, and living floor mop. They come with open arms and begging for hugs in one moment, and they elude us, giggling, to hide from kisses in the next. Sometimes proud to please, often defying to tease, adventuring without fear to the extremities of their capabilities and our discomfort, they try their wings and our patience. Bumps and bruises, skinned knees and noses are a part of their daily fare. As John and I look back, we wonder with gratitude to God that our six survived so well the multitude of normal toddling terrors—as do most parents.

Physical hurts are easily ministered to with kisses that really do "make it well" and by magic Band-Aids, piggyback rides, and cookies while we rock and sing the wounded one to sleep. Nap time seems to accomplish a forgetting of minor accidents and injuries. After a good sleep the toddler will bubble up into unbelievably fresh and vigorous activity, whether propelled on all fours or on legs that always seem too short to keep up with the enthusiastic thrust of curiosity running pell-mell. Such vigor, enthusiasm, and curiosity need encouragement to grow, plus loving discipline to provide limits that become security for the toddler. He is the center of his own world emotionally and experimentally and knows nothing yet of the magnitude of challenges and challengers to be encountered.

John and I have sometimes tried to put ourselves imaginatively in a toddler's position to gain his point of view—a world of knees, enormous behinds, tall and tiny heads that always seem to be jabbering strange noises toward us. We're supposed to respond to those confusing sounds. There is one sound that comes again and again—"No, no!" Often that sound comes with a shout, a scowl, and inflicted pain. And we wonder why. What we were doing *felt* so good! We do that thing again, and we experience repeated displeasure from the people who stand four times our height.

We soon learn to associate an act we do with the pain that comes through the huge hands of the tall people. The pain is called "no-no." Those hands are the same hands that feed us, give us loving strokes, and pick us up when we fall. So we quickly learn to measure the "feeling good," which the doing of "no-no" brings, against the price of the momentary pain of the slap on our backside. We understand the light pain. It brings cause and effect to sharp and simple focus, though it elicits a tearful, angry response. A tirade of angry words throws us into confusion; we feel compelled to respond to directions that are to us a mystery. Equally untranslatable is "sweet reasonableness"; it sugarcoats the angry energies we feel rushing toward us. We are frightened. We rush into the big arms and hands that sometimes give loving strokes and demand acceptance. If we are rebuked, we flee wounded into tears or temper. But soon we learn to gain the best of two worlds. We can do the "no-no" when no one is looking!

Identifying so with the toddler, it is easy to see how qualities of self-preservation and manipulation are born in normal healthy families and nurtured by responsible, caring parents who only do what they *can* do. *If* there were a way to be a perfect parent, it would be impossible to raise a perfect child. After all, God is a perfect Father, and every child of His except our Lord Jesus fell so badly as to need a Savior!

Before consciousness of right and wrong is developed or conscience is activated, we "sin" for personal gratification or to gain advantage. By the time we grow into consciousness and conscience, we have already developed deeply ingrained habit patterns of manipulation, control, striving, sneaking, and lying. They form without our knowing it in the motivational foundations in us by which we do all we do—sometimes wrong things for wrong motives, and sometimes good things from either good or wrong motives. Most often, until prayer ministry intervenes, we remain unaware of our real motivations. The Lord Jesus must therefore redeem and transform to the depths of our hidden foundations.

One of the primary tasks a toddler must learn is to control his bladder and bowels. A mother understandably looks forward to the end of dirty diapers. But if she is so anxious to arrive at freedom, she may push the child into a discipline of bowel control he is neither physically nor emotionally prepared to handle. She may build into her child habits of striving, structures of rigidity, and attitudes of fastidiousness that limit his freedom to be and to express who he is. These structures will find what are called "anal" expressions in him in adulthood.

A mother may express great pride that her six-month-old was potty trained, when in truth the mother has been trained to anticipate time patterns and recognize symptoms of the approaching need to eliminate. Such a mother has imposed her training on the child, at great cost to the child. Often in such a case ego involvement is expressed strongly when her child, not trained at all, has an "accident." "Shame on you! Oh, nasty! *Phew!* Bad! Dirty!" At that point the child may begin to view his body and its normal functions as something shameful and to be despised. This may become an unconscious part of his foundational attitude toward his body and, more pertinently, toward his sexuality.

More devastating to a toddler is pressure that confuses love with performance. The child has just done a successful job on the pot. Thinking to encourage, the mother says, "You did good! Mommy is proud of you! Mommy *loves* you!" The child needs recognition for having succeeded, but never should performance be associated with love, or failure be rewarded by lack of loving expression. Love must be poured out unconditionally, especially to undergird and encourage the child to venture in his learning of new skills.

The toddler who stands humiliated and rejected with a malodorous lump in his britches and loudly proclaims, "I didn't do it!" may be one and the same with the adult who cannot admit his mistakes because he cannot feel loved as one who has failed.

Or he may be the man who unconsciously retreats from his wife, avoiding more than surface sharing, because he cannot at the root level of his being believe that the woman would be sensitive to him in his imperfections. He is afraid to allow himself to be vulnerable because of the specter of his mother—the screaming voice, the biting tongue, and the accusing finger. He may have made a deep inner vow never to be "found out," and so strives to maintain a façade of macho-niceness and self-sufficiency, while actually dying inside due to the absence of real intimacy.

To exhort such an adult to trust, to be open and truthful, to relax, and to make himself vulnerable is to insist that he do what he has been structured and tutored *not* to do! He may try, but his early fears will rise from the depths of his inner being to prevent him, triggered by no more than mildly impatient prodding by his wife.

If a man has been strongly taught to feel loved only when fulfilling a confused need to perform well, any exhortation will throw him into self-defeating striving. The more he tries to relax, the tenser he will become as he strives to succeed. The more he tries to be open and truthful, the more he will control and judge his success or failure. When he fails, as he must sooner or later, the more frantic he will become to cover it in order to be accepted. "Don't tell me I'm not doing it right!"

HEALING THE HURTS EXPERIENCED DURING TODDLER YEARS

These types of examples are very familiar to many of us, and if we are to receive effective ministry in this area, it must speak to those places in our hearts that still hurt as if we are still that child being scolded, those parts of our hearts that still feed us with anxiety and imprison us in childish emotions. Jesus came to set prisoners free. He is the only one who can reach to those deep parts of our hearts and enable us to forgive and be forgiven. He is the only one who can "create in me a clean heart, O God, and renew a steadfast spirit within me" (Ps. 51:10). "When I was a child, I talked like a child, I thought like a child, I reasoned like a child. When I became a man, I put childish ways behind me" (1 Cor. 13:11, NIV). That maturation waits upon a gift of power from the Lord, usually needing to be ministered to us by loving people; otherwise we cannot accomplish that "putting away."

When receiving prayer or ministry, the part of your heart that still hurts from childhood wounds needs to hear again and again that you are not loved more if you do it right, nor any less if you do it wrong, whatever the "it" is. You need to apprehend as a personal reality that you are loved by our Lord *unconditionally*, at all times, no matter how well or poorly you perform.

FIRM, LOVING DISCIPLINE BUILDS A CHILD

Our grandson Nathan, when he was not yet three, was extremely independent and willful and quite fond of peanut butter. His mother, Beth, left him alone with his peanut butter sandwich one day, with strict instructions to leave his bib on. Nathan had noticed that older people do not eat with bibs. Anxious to be an older person himself, he promptly removed his bib. Beth returned to find that Nathan had completed his lunch, but peanut butter was everywhere—all over his hands, face, shirt, table, and chair! Before she could say a word he blurted out, "Ise clean! Ise clean!" She took him firmly in hand, slapped him on the behind, and lovingly marched him off to the bathroom, saying gently but firmly, "You are not clean. You disobeyed and ate without your bib. Now we'll have to wash you and your clothes."

She called him to account. She brought discipline to momentary painful focus with the light spanking. But she in no way withheld her love from him. Neither did she humiliate or rail at him.

Firm discipline in love builds basic abilities in toddlers by which as adults they will be able to confess to the Father God or to another human being, "I've done wrong. Forgive me. Let me make amends." But a childhood base of rejection and humiliation may cause a person to rationalize, lie, cover his tracks, and always be on the defensive—until the cross of Christ brings the old way of the child in him to death and gives birth to a new way of thinking, feeling, and acting. "Truly, truly, I say to you, unless one is born again, he cannot see the kingdom of God" (John 3:3). The kingdom of God is secondarily a place; it is primarily a way of relating to God and to one another without guile and without shame.

Consistent, firm discipline provides a toddler with the assurance that he will not be allowed to run amok. Having that, he can rest securely and be unafraid to venture. Loving discipline blends firmly with acceptance. Love tempers consistency of discipline to prevent rigidity so that discipline is appropriate to the occasion and to the changing needs of the toddler.

My little brother, Norman, was told to stay away from the old wringer-type washing machine. His curiosity, along with his desire to be as big as the rest of us who were helping our mother, got the best of him. His arm was caught in the wringer and pulled in up to his armpit. Disobedience by general principle would have been rewarded with gentle scolding or spanking. Neither was in order here. He had clearly already reaped the reward of that particular disobedience.

Further discipline would not have been discipline at all, but cruel punishment. The primary purpose of discipline is not to punish but to structure. The message already built into his inner being that day was, "When you disobey the rules laid down by those who by experience know more than you do, you get into painful trouble. When you are hurting, you are not condemned for being what you are, but you are met and loved and healed by the very ones who gave you the warning in the first place." Is not that the way parents should communicate the nature of God before children have the intellectual capacity to comprehend? "He will call upon Me, and I will answer him" (Ps. 91:15). Children cannot abstract. They experience *particular,* specific pains and joys. God comes to them through the hands of parents.

Parents who vent their emotions on a child who is already terrified and "bleeding" communicate an altogether different sort of message to his heart. They bind him to his pain in condemnation for having done a "stupid" thing. As adults we need to be free to risk doing things that might turn out to be stupid. We need to be free to say yes or no from our own individual center of decision inside ourselves and to reap the consequences of our choices without condemnation. God calls us to be sons, not robots. Emotionally or physically battered children are seldom capable of freedom that enables wise choices as adults.

While we are yet toddlers, we are practicing to be free. Of course, toddlers must be controlled and protected. They have not gained by experience the wisdom to keep from killing themselves and others. Witness a fifteen-month-old who sinks his teeth into his friend's arm and registers surprise at the reaction. But our controlling behavior must never completely squelch the toddler's courage to say no or to express his displeasure. A teenager who has ego strength to say no to his peers is one who as a toddler was allowed freedom to say no without being condemned and who was also not allowed by the no to run willfully over authority.

I (Paula) was seated on the couch one afternoon. At the end of the couch was a table that held one of my favorite houseplants. Our grandson Jason, then not yet two, began to stir in the dirt with his fingers. I said, "No, Jason." He withdrew his fingers quickly, watched me intently for a few moments, and deliberately stuck his hand back in the dirt and began to squeeze whole handfuls. I took his hand out, brushed the dirt from his fingers, and repeated a firm, "No! No! No!" He quickly repeated the aggressive action, and I slapped his hand. He stepped back, clenched both his fists, screwed up his face, shrieked one long, disapproving screech, and then came to sit on my lap. The matter was settled. I felt no compulsion to punish him for screeching what was on his mind. He never again ventured to play in my potted plants. As an adult today, he is very much his own person, has respect for authority, and still loves to "play in the dirt" when and where it is appropriate, like football on a muddy field.

Sometimes toddlers say no not because they mean no but just to delight in the privilege of saying the word. Our children loved things like car rides, romping on the floor with daddy, and ice cream. Sometimes as toddlers, when offered one of these experiences, they would practice saying no and then happily enjoy it anyway. We knew they didn't mean no. With all of our six children we went through periods when they were toddlers of playing games of "saying"—just for fun.

"Yes," we would begin.

"No," they would respond.

"Yes," we would insist.

"No," they would return emphatically.

We would change our response to no—and they'd change with a giggle to yes.

Just as they learned by the peekaboo game that we could move out of sight and return again, and that it was OK to trust, so they learned by the "yes-no" game that it was all right to express an opposing opinion. They would not be rejected for being different. That did not guarantee that our children would always stand against peer pressure later. They did their share of sinning, but the basic structure of freedom to choose was in them, and in those areas warped by our mistakes, the Lord's grace was there to redeem and remold.

As the years progressed, we learned that the best and most effective prayer to bring our children into tune with the purposes of God was to pray as St. Paul did, that they be strengthened with power and might in the inner man (Eph. 3:16). That is another way of saying, "Lord, set them free from all bondage—even my anxiety for them—and give them root-level courage to make good choices and to become who *they are* in You, not just what I want them to be."

DAMAGED EQUIPMENT

But suppose that as adults we discover that our freedom to be and to express freely was damaged or destroyed in the beginning.

Bud was one of the "nicest" people I have ever met. He would bend over backward to do anything to help someone. He would never say a bad word about anybody. Yet he continually struggled with anger. He was driven to find the "right" way to do things, and though he would never express it, he had little patience with those who didn't perform according to standard. But he could never vent his frustrations openly—except to his wife, who received the brunt of all he had suppressed inside. Then he would condemn himself for those outbursts. He struggled with sexual lusts, had some difficulty with voyeurism, and found it a strain to relate to women, especially to sweet women. The more his wife related to him lovingly and forgivingly, the more upset he became. As we talked with him and sought the Lord's wisdom about how to pray, we found that Bud had been controlled from the time he was a little child by the sweet, smothering, manipulative reasonableness of his mother.

"No, Bud. We don't want to feel that way, do we?"

"We aren't going to do that, are we?"

"Now, honey, nice boys don't stomp their feet."

"Honey, you don't want to hurt Mommy by doing that, do you?" Of course he wanted to do that thing, but "sweet" mommy manipulated him out of it.

He had never learned to respectfully articulate contrary thoughts and feelings and work them through to resolution. Instead, he had learned to stuff down every real, rotten impulse he had, including his hatred for his mother—who had never allowed him to be himself! His sense of humor had completely died, if it had ever lived.

The first order of ministry was to pray for that time in his heart when he had been manipulated as a little child. He needed to be taken through a process where he could forgive and be forgiven. Then he needed prayer for love to cast out fear. We asked the Lord to lift off of the little boy the oppressive burden of performing and to set him free inside to be himself. "Lord, take away the dread seriousness of life and give to Bud the freedom to goof and to laugh at himself—to stomp his foot, say a nasty word, get dirt all over his clothes, and know that You're still there with open arms and an understanding heart." We persisted in those prayers and saw the Lord accomplish resurrection in Bud. He even learned to laugh at what he had been like.

Toddlers are naturally all curiosity and full of adventure— exploring, tasting, testing, finding out what their bodies can and can't do. Each one is different. One cannot stamp a principle on every toddler and make it work. Each has to be met and dealt with as a unique person. We used to pursue our little ones to the edge of the dock, or haul them back out of traffic, or catch them as they jumped off the back porch, breathlessly wondering if they'd make it to voting age.

At eighteen months Loren thought nothing of plunging head-long into Lake Michigan. He'd seen his father do it many times, and after all, wasn't it wet like the water we had such fun splashing in at home? With equal abandon he would rush down any street or alley in pursuit of flocks of pigeons. "Look at de birds! Look at de birds!"

With Ami in a stroller, Loren so full of spontaneous enthusiasm, and my hands full of groceries, I learned that it was best to put him in a body harness in busy downtown Chicago and attach him to the stroller lest he have some sudden inspiration to leave us on the first departing elevated train. From little old ladies who did not know

Loren as well as we did, this brought many looks of, "What's the matter with that mother?"

When Loren was ten and a half months old, a neighbor in our apartment house at the University of Chicago opened the door for him (because "he looked like he knew where he was going"), and we found him across the street on the second floor fire escape of the veteran's student housing. A few months later it happened again, and someone found him on the nearby Midway Plaisance and turned him in to the Rockefeller Chapel office. He was unconcerned as we picked him up. He knew where he was; he'd been there before.

Ami was more conservative. She stuck her foot into a basement drain, and for a while we thought we'd have to get a jackhammer to extract her. But at least we knew where she was. On the other hand, on hot days she thought nothing of removing all of her clothes to make the most of the breezes; the neighbors all called her "Crinkle Buns."

With Mark we had a respite. He was content to spend hours playing in a corner, studying pictures in a magazine, chasing birds of thought, and exploring inner space. But he could be active when he wanted. He would run from the cat until the cat took a flying leap to get a claw hold in Mark's drooping diapers. And they'd sprawl together with him giggling and leaping to do it again.

Then came Johnny. He stood up in his crib at five months, took his first step at nine months, and immediately tacked on thirty-nine more until he wound up swinging from a drape in the living room, and from then on he was undaunted. We thought about billing him as the "human fly"; he could climb anything—and usually did.

Timothy, at age three, fell in the men's restroom at a campground in British Columbia (because he wanted "to do it himself") and cleanly extracted four front teeth when his mouth hit the toilet bowl.

Andrea came along in our later years, and the Lord had mercy and gave us another quiet one who, like her sister, was happy to explore cupboards and flush things down the toilet rather than occupy herself with more dangerous pursuits. The only time I remember being really upset with Andrea as a toddler was the day she and her little friend decided to decorate the bedroom wall with a large crayon mural. They were so proud of the job they had done and so perplexed by our not-too-controlled rage!

We wrote all of the above to say that each child is different. Don't try to stamp them in the same mold; what works for one may not work for another. Rejoice, as God does, in the variety.

Over the years we have appreciated more and more of the wisdom of the Lord in giving us our children while we are young and, for most of us, one at a time. At the same time we grieve for those modern-day young people who flee from the responsibility or the discomfort of raising children. We look at those years as being rich and exciting, if oftentimes frightening, and know that with each child we gained a new dimension of the capacity to live and to give and receive blessing.

RESIST THE URGE TO OVERPROTECT

The temptation we all must check as parents is the urge to overprotect. There is a fine line between mothering and smothering, fathering and bothering. We have known adults who have never been able to enjoy the delicious freedom of walking barefoot in the cool grass or stretching their bare toes in front of the TV after a hard day's work because as children they were made to feel guilty for taking off their shoes. "You might step on something and cut your feet!"

Some grown-ups have a fear of heights for no other reason than that they were never allowed to climb trees or play in tree houses. "Be careful! You might fall!" Many people live out their lives with a fear of animals because of repeated warnings, "Don't go near dogs! They might bite!" And some never get over the fear to venture into new experiences because of continuous refrains of "You're too little to do that." "Here, let me do that for you." "Watch out!" "What makes you think you can ride that bike?" "Let somebody who knows how do it." "You'll get lost." Thinking to save life, overprotective parents snuff it out, projecting their fears into their children. They actually are protecting their own comfort zone.

What *can* we do that we might shepherd our children in their adventures? We need to get at those things in our flesh that feed our own fears, call to death in prayer our needs to control and manipulate, and ask for wisdom to "train up a child in the way *he* should go" (Prov. 22:6, emphasis added; in the Hebrew, "according to the way of him," that is, according to his own natural bent). Again, for the adult whose fears of risking are rooted in reactions to overcontrolling parents—the way to freedom is always to forgive the sin against you, to be forgiven your response to that sin, to be given a new heart and a gift of trust, and finally to be loosed to live and laugh, run and risk.

In our book *Restoring the Christian Family*, we devote an entire chapter, "A Place for Fantasy," to the subject of shepherding the imagination of a child. Suffice it here to say that the imagination of a toddler is very active. His spiritual sensitivity is keen, and he is often aware of spiritual realities adults have long ago tuned out. A toddler may cry out in the middle of the night that someone is in his room and that he is afraid. He may have dreamed, he may be imagining, or he may really sense a demonic presence there. It is not so important that we determine the cause of his fear as it is for us to stand *with* him in his fear with quiet confidence that Jesus is there to protect and overcome in all circumstances. By our manner we will communicate that there is nothing to fear. We can also communicate that by simple prayer.

If we ridicule the child's perceptions, we undermine his confidence in his ability to see. If we express anger at his insistence, we will thereby be telling him we cannot be trusted to understand, accept, and help him to overcome the enemies he finds in the dark. But if we respect his realities and invite the Lord into them as one before whom every knee in heaven and on the earth must bow (Phil. 2:10–11), we will instill confidence in the child that God is always at hand, understanding, ready, and more than adequate to overcome all that threatens. The Lord who descended into hell and led a host captive (1 Pet. 3:19; Eph. 4:8) will certainly have no trouble banishing shadows from a nursery wall, be they real or imagined.

Like the disciples who tried to keep little children from bothering Jesus, many people would brush toddlers aside, not realizing that the deepest lessons of life are learned in the early years in the tiniest, often most repetitive details.

In the church we often put children who are less than three years old with babysitters who have no awareness or inclination to teach because we are too unaware of a child's capacity to learn at that most pliable and sensitive age. We should put our most loving, creative teachers with the little ones! I remember most clearly a class of two-year-olds I once taught. We climbed into a boat (the table) with Jesus one Sunday, and the storm came and the boat rocked and some were so afraid that they actually started to cry. And then we all imagined Jesus awakening and speaking from our "boat" to calm the storm. After the storm had settled, we all thanked Jesus for taking such good care of us. Years later, one of those now-adult children recalled to me the vividness of that experience.

When a death occurs in the family, sometimes everyone assumes too glibly that a baby or toddler is too little to understand, so he is left alone to absorb the energies of the family's grief with no one to minister sensitively to his feelings of loss and confusion. He cannot yet intellectualize, but his little spirit is most certainly aware. In times of bereavement, in the busy world of adults, even the normal fare of hugs for little ones may be neglected.

There are other kinds of losses, significant to a toddler but lost to us grown-ups. A favorite toy is run over in the driveway. "It's only a toy. He'll get over it." A pet is hit by a car. "Don't worry about it. Get him another puppy. He won't even remember it next week." Parents are fighting. The toddler hears and, more importantly, feels the tearing between his parents. They do not realize that his base of security is being ripped from under him, that in his spirit he may be pulled apart as they separate. "He's too little to understand." No, a thousand times no! He is more sensitive then than he will ever be, and he needs loving shepherding of his imagination and feelings.

FRACTURED EMOTIONS

In the first year of a child's life, basic trust is gained or it isn't. Basic trust is the capacity to hold the heart open, to risk in sustained heart-to-heart involvement with imperfect people. Basic trust is the inner strength and resilience necessary to human relationships, the capacity to remain vulnerable to people who cannot always be trusted.

If a little child were to fall and break a leg, and if that leg failed to mend well, he would go limping through life. We can see that fracture and its cause and easily sympathize. But emotional wounds are as real as broken legs, and a child may go limping throughout life because of them. Such fractures cannot be seen except by the X-ray of Holy Spirit insight. Not seeing, people tend to be less aware and compassionate. Repeated wounding and repeated sinful reactions to hurts result in character-structure habits, ways of responding to life in defensive or hurtfully aggressive actions. We need to have our eyes opened to the terrible fact that a great many of the practices in our carnal character, with which we struggle so fiercely, were formed in our first two or three years on the earth! Once we fully come to comprehend the awesomeness of that fact, our hearts and minds will be easily filled with our Lord's gentle compassion.

The assurance we have in the Word of God that "surely our griefs He Himself bore and our sorrows He carried" (Isa. 53:4) is not only for present ills but also for all our yesterdays, all the way back to our beginnings. Jesus Christ is able to touch, heal, and transform *all* that has gone on before, *all* that has shaped us, *all* that has driven us from within the hidden places in our hearts since our first years. He does not erase the past. He transforms every experience of our lives into strength, understanding, compassion, and instruments of healing—from the very substance of our former wounds and the humiliation that our sins have caused.

CHAPTER 5

SOCIAL GROWTH AND INTERACTION

Train up a child in the way he should go, even when he is
old he will not depart from it.

—PROVERBS 22:6

The most common responses from anxious parents to
Proverbs 22:6 are: "I want to believe that, but how old does
the child have to be before he stops departing!" "If that's
true, then where did we go wrong?" "We gave Susie everything! She
doesn't appreciate anything!" Missing from all those comments is
basic understanding of what we consider to be the key word in the
scripture, "Train up a child in the way *he* should go."

The original Hebrew rendering of Proverbs 22:6 literally reads,
"Train the child according to the way of *him*, and when he is old,
he will not turn from *him*." Who does "him" refer to? Proverbs
are popular sayings voiced in isolation of each other that have
been compiled on the same pages merely for the reader's conve-
nience. Therefore, unlike all other scriptures, each proverb has

no context. There is nothing outside this verse that reveals who "him" represents. So the antecedent for "him" must be found within the proverb itself. That leaves only one possibility—the child ("Train up a child according to the way of *him* [the child], and when he is old, he will not turn from *him* [himself]"). Therefore, parents are not to impose their own selfish agenda on the child. He is not a *tabula rasa* (blank slate) on which they can stamp whatever they wish. From conception, God has inlaid in him his own individual design, waiting to be discovered, developed, and nurtured by discerning and observant parents.

The important thing is to discover the way *he* should go, according to the *Lord's* purposes for him, and lovingly, sensitively, invitingly train him so as to set him free to become the most God has created him to be. "For we are His workmanship, created in Christ Jesus *for* good works, which God prepared beforehand, that we should walk in them" (Eph. 2:10, emphasis added).

God's peculiar preparation of good works for our son or daughter may or may not coincide with our family traditions. "We hoped Jimmy would be a lawyer like his father and his father before him." God's plan may run totally counter to our dreaming, hoping, and planning: "But I always dreamed of having a doctor in the family!" But "love does not insist on its own way" (1 Cor. 13:5, RSV). To superimpose even the noblest aspirations on our children is not love.

I (Paula) firmly believe that each and every person is created for good works and uniquely equipped for those by seeds of natural interest and talent implanted by God. He is not limited by these, for God can broaden any person to do a specific task by enabling him to learn new skills to meet needs. But that which most restfully fulfills a person and enables him to most fruitfully and joyfully contribute is for him to be seen, respectfully met, and nurtured in his own natural gifts by parents and teachers. If a child is thus trained in the way he should go, it will feel so right, *Prov 22:6* rewarding, and fulfilling. He will be at home in it. The way will be a part of him, and he a part of it. And he will not depart from it.

A friend of ours, Roger Youmans, MD, a former associate professor of surgery at Oral Roberts University Medical School, shared with us this definition of *health*: "Health is that relationship between an organism and its environment which enables the organism to fulfill its purpose." Love in a family, like education in a school, should be designed to produce healthy human organisms. By Roger's definition, a child who has been conformed to fulfill purposes not his own is not a healthy organism. He may go limping through life striving to please people but never doing what he was designed by God to do. He may be shriveling inside for fear of failure and rejection. He may be overcome with shame for not living up to expectations. He may be polluting the spiritual atmosphere by sins of rebellious anger and resentment for never being accepted for who he is, rather than only for the role he has consented to play.

Prayer for the healing of the inner man always involves at root a decision to forgive, a plea to be forgiven, and a discipline of walking in the new life. The purpose of healing is not to enable a person to do successfully what others have wanted him to do all along. It is not merely to make him feel better. It is to restore a person to the original purpose for which he was created, to gift him with the courage to become. It is therefore to set him free from judgment, condemnation, and fear about what others think of him.

That is not a complicated process. It is a simple matter of recognizing that a part of the house of our life is weak and crumbling or filled with unhappiness and strife because there is a serious defect in the foundation of character upon which our house was built. We are told in Luke 6 to dig deep and lay our foundation on the Rock (who is Jesus) so that when the floods of life arise, we will be able to stand, whatever pressure hits us.

> The good man out of the good treasure of his heart brings forth what is good; and the evil man out of the evil treasure brings forth what is evil; for his mouth speaks from that which fills his heart. And why do you call Me, "Lord, Lord," and do not do what I say? Everyone who comes to Me, and hears My words, and acts upon them, I will show you whom he is like: he is like a man building a house, who dug deep and laid a foundation upon the rock; and when a flood rose, the torrent burst against that house and could not shake it, because it had been well built. But the one who has heard, and has not acted accordingly, is like a man who built a house upon the ground without any foundation; and the torrent burst against it and immediately it collapsed, and the ruin of that house was great.
>
> —Luke 6:45–49

Often we recognize that our lives are expressing actions and attitudes that do not manifest a good treasure in the heart. If we neglect to search out the rottenness in some of our foundation stones (the early years of our life upon which all the subsequent years of our life are built) to allow the Lord to transform those stones into the solid substance of His own nature, it will be only a matter of time before the pressures of responsibility and the

difficulties of circumstances (the floods of great waters) bring us
to spiritual, emotional, and physical cave-ins and washouts.

The following stories illustrate many of the kinds of flaws in
foundation stones that occur in preschool and early school years.

How to Bury Your Children With Their Talents

Eugene was the first of two children. Fearful for the safety of
their little boy, his parents determined to protect him from all
harm. He was not allowed to leave his yard to play with a friend.
Neighborhood children were not made to feel welcome in his
home. Playtime was never carefree because mother was always
interfering. Messes were not tolerated. He was never allowed
to ride a bicycle or to roar down the sidewalk on roller skates.
When he started school, his mother walked him to the school-
yard every day, then met him and saw to it that he arrived home
safely. This continued into third grade. By then he was allowed to
leave his yard, but he had no friends.

He continued as a loner throughout his school career and
did poorly in his studies despite volumes of "help" lavished by
a mother who had no idea she was undermining his confidence
by her overprotectiveness and unspoken messages that told him:
"You couldn't get along without me." When he married, he was
unable to hold a job and became dependent on his wife, first for
every emotional and then material support. He became an alco-
holic to comfort the insecurity he felt about himself as a man.
He was also mildly agoraphobic (fear of open spaces), always
fearful about traveling more than a few miles off familiar paths.
He accepted the Lord in a real born-again experience but was

too embarrassed to let himself be known by becoming part of a church. He never grew up in his salvation (1 Pet. 2:2).

Jealousy prevented the development of a relationship between him and his younger brother, who seemed to be determined to be his own person and to succeed no matter what.

Eugene died at an early age, never having developed the outstanding gift for writing and storytelling with which the Lord had equipped him from the beginning.

> For to everyone who has shall more be given, and he shall have an abundance; but from the one who does not have, even what he does have shall be taken away.
> —MATTHEW 25:29

In Eugene's case it was not that only a few of his foundation stones were flawed. It was that his life had been built on the quicksand of having had everything done for him, of never having been allowed to exercise his own muscles of responsibility that would have developed in him a measure of self-confidence. Whatever spirit of adventure he might have had in the beginning was so bound by parental fears and controls that he lost all courage to risk. Healing for him would have only begun with forgiveness. Then he would have needed continual prayer and association with others who could call him forth to life. Being born anew, he needed others to support and affirm his coming forth by spending time with him, completely rebuilding his foundations through the expressed love of Jesus in daily actions. But his carnal conditioning overcame him—he fled from life. His condition is called amniosis, a habit of fleeing back to the "safe" amniotic environment of the womb.

SIBLING SUFFERINGS

> We also exult in our tribulations; knowing that tribulation brings
> about perseverance; and perseverance, proven character; and
> proven character, hope.
>
> —ROMANS 5:3–4

As adults we tend to look upon the trials and upsets of small children as being relatively unimportant immaturities that will soon pass. Or being discomfited by their quarrels and tears, we may ignore them altogether, ridicule their silliness, or rush in to settle matters prematurely. We need to realize that the tiny tribulations of a young child are mountainous to him, and his emotions all-consuming. The events with which he struggles may soon fall into forgetfulness, but the reactions of primary people to his handling of events become a part of the storehouse of his heart and continue all his life to influence him from within.

A young child has not yet developed faculties to think through his experiences to put them in a context of past and future. He hurts now as if this moment is all there is and vents the steam of hurt as an appeal for immediate comfort and aid.

For instance, Joey has spent considerable time building a tall tower with his blocks. He leaves the room to get his mother to look and admire. While he is gone, little brother knocks the entire construction down and gleefully sits on it. Mother consoles Joey and gives him an ice cream cone, which the dog grabs out of his hand, and in his urgency to save his treat from the thief, he trips over little brother and the pile of blocks and falls to the floor, hitting his head on the corner of a chair. Hurt and rage need a place to land, so he pops baby brother with a block. To Joey that series of events is as devastating an experience as that of a grown man who, after hours of hard work, loses a coveted business deal because of the bungling of an inept colleague, then makes a recovery, only to lose credit for it due to misrepresentation by one of the company "glory boys" who hops on the bandwagon at the last minute.

In either case, the outraged cry of "It's not fair" needs to be met with sensitivity before teaching. If Joey's mother only punishes him for lashing out, she will feed in him a judgment about not being understood, about being pushed aside in favor of the younger brother, and about being given a raw deal by those he is supposed to be able to trust. As adults, many of us have trouble with "brothers" in business or in organizational groups. We may have stones at the base of our foundations that bear the imprint of many such incidents with natural brothers and sisters. We may have judged, hated, and built bitter expectations, and now we are reaping. *as we continue to* Bury the anger *pain, disappoint-ment, blame*

JEALOUSIES

Marilyn's husband is leaving her for another woman, her best friend. She feels betrayed, rejected, ugly, and worthless. Prayer ministry reveals that from the time her younger sister was born, *or older* Marilyn felt second best—not as pretty, talented, or lovable. Her mom and dad seemed always to be giving her sister advantages. She protests that she loves her sister, but her sister was *other* the one whom friends always called first, the one who had all the boyfriends, won all the awards, and so on. Others in the family remember Marilyn's history differently than she does. They knew the animosity. Marilyn needs to see her bitter-root judgment and expectancy to be aced out by another and forgive her sister and all who seemed to favor her. She needs to prayerfully connect with the hurt she still experiences as a result of those childhood events. She needs to allow Jesus into those places in her heart so that He can reveal to her the truth about herself and enable her to let go of judgments she made in relation to her sister, her parents, God, and herself. The Lord can then help her to grow into an appreciative awareness of her own beauty and worth in Him.

Not all childhood judgments we make concerning siblings become a lasting part of us. My (Paula's) brothers, Jerry and Stan, were born twenty months apart. They enjoyed many early adventures together, including a lot of healthy rough-and-tumble. When Jerry, the older, started school, Stan naturally thought he should be allowed to go also. When he was denied that privilege, he was angry with Jerry, thinking it was Jerry's fault. Apparently he nursed that blame for at least a year, for when he was allowed to enter kindergarten, he insisted on walking to school on the opposite side of the street from Jerry. But the misunderstanding took no deep root. A part of that is probably due to our parents, who could arbitrate lovingly with no partiality. A large part was due to choices the boys made at that early age to forgive and choose one another. They remain good friends to this day, and each has succeeded well in his own field.

Our choices play a great part in determining whether tribulation ultimately produces character and hope. No amount of counsel or prayer for inner healing can change our hearts if we have not yet made a choice deep down to let go of what lies behind and press on toward what lies ahead (Phil. 3:13–15). Healing comes to us when we become determined not to "use" the events of our lives to excuse ourselves or to prove others wrong.

ECONOMIC DOWNS AND HAND-ME-DOWNS

We have ministered to many who were small children during the Great Depression and post-depression years. We found two major reactions to their common experience of compulsory frugality. Some continue to nurse feelings of deprivation and try to compensate with periodic buying sprees. Or they have determined not to let their children go without as they had to do, splurging too much for them. They are offended by the offer of hand-me-downs. "I never had anything new that I could call my own! I'm going to see that my children have the very best!"

Others in depression times seem to have developed a keen ability to determine the difference between want and need, a talent for using scrap materials creatively, and an appreciation for bargains and shared resources. Sometimes they will need prayer before they can buy for themselves or accept luxurious gifts without vague guilt feelings, but they are not driven to excesses to fill emotional pits of deprivation. The difference lies again in the quality of the foundation stones. (Train up a child in any way at all, and until something enters his life to change it, he will not depart from it.)

If a child was given plenty of affection, if his family unit stayed together, if there was an absence of quarreling, if sharing was expressed as sacrificial love, if there were games and fun times in the family, a small child's occasional hurts probably will not lodge as destructive patterns of reaping in adulthood. On the other hand, for example, in families in which financial stress was allowed to overcome love, to warp harmony, and to break unity, their small children most likely absorbed anxiety, and the resulting insecurity became a part of their basic attitudes toward life.

In both poor and affluent families, the story is usually the same where there are many children. Hand-me-downs naturally come to the younger members. In one family the younger children are proud to wear big brother's or sister's outgrown clothes; it may symbolize to them that they too are maturing into the image of their sibling heroes. Or if the siblings are not heroes to them, they may respond jealously or angrily to being treated like second best. What goes into the storehouse of the heart to wound or bless is *not the event or circumstance itself, but always the individual's reaction to it.* Second-best mentality in the heart can rise to find expression in many ways throughout life—expectation to be bypassed for job promotions or awards, inability to believe one's own mate chooses him above all others, reticence to put oneself forward to serve or to claim one's place, awkwardness in response to compliments, difficulty even to believe that "Jesus loves *me*," and so on. Seeing a trauma in childhood, we do not automatically expect some kind of adverse reaping in adulthood. But it does work the other way around. Seeing a harmful pattern in adulthood, we look for something congruent in the childhood. We track from fruits to roots.

Belonging—Confusion and Exclusion

A child commences to move into his peer group when he leaves the familiar protected surroundings of his home and begins to venture into his and the neighbors' yards to play. He soon begins to experience a confusing disparity between the way his mom and dad act and the way things are done down the block. For instance, he learns a strange new vocabulary that wins him approval among his peers but is rewarded with soap in the mouth when he uses it at home! He finds himself wrestling with questions of justice when he is spanked for violations of rules and his friend is not. I (Paula) remember when our son Loren, then four or five, ran down the alley with his friend Ernie; the two of them plucked ripe tomatoes and threw them for the fun of the splat against the neighbors' wall. Loren was spanked and required to apologize to the neighbors; Ernie was not. Loren was outraged.

Peer-group loyalties take an increasingly firm hold on every child, and a wise parent will relate sympathetically to pressures on the child while administering appropriate discipline to build in solid, healthy value systems. A child may react with violent emotions to what at the moment he considers to be unfair. But if sensitivity and love are expressed concurrently with whatever the shape of discipline, that will serve as good mortar base for the laying of solid foundation stones.

If judgments are made against parents for excessive (or perceived as excessive) discipline, forgiveness can be accomplished later. But lack of discipline leaves a child without bounds for his energies and drives, and this results in more than a need for inner healing as an adult. At some point he will have to be given what was not given; someone will have to give him some form of discipline as a parent in Christ, else he will flounder and err forever without structure. He will not have self-limits built within him to know when he is trampling on others or taking unfair advantage. He will be vulnerable to the urgencies of the moment, unable to easily take into account the dynamics of cause and effect. "Like a city that is broken into and without walls is a man who has no control over his spirit" (Prov. 25:28). Frequently we have prayed with people to enable them to forgive parents for not disciplining them. A child's mind may shout hallelujah for "getting by" with a transgression, while his heart feels unloved and afraid.

Every child has a tremendous need to be accepted among his peers. Our oldest son demonstrated this dramatically in the early 1950s when we were living in the University of Chicago community. The students in our seminary housing took great delight in Loren's ability as a two-year-old to mimic the current theological vocabulary without missing a syllable. As he played in the front yard of Kimbark House, many students and teachers going to and from classes would stop and chat with our little towhead. Because of his facility in conversation, they were invariably astonished to learn that he was so young.

It was not long before Loren was attracted to the far end of the block where many children played in a courtyard area behind a group of apartment houses. He had been given a little blue tricycle, and daily he would pedal down the sidewalk in search of playmates. Again and again he would return in tears because of the taunts of the children: "You're a dummy! You don't even know how old you are!" It was difficult for them to believe that one who rode and spoke in such a grown-up manner could be only two years old. We would hug him and wipe his tears, and he would return once more to try to become a part of the group he referred to as the "roughie toughies." That effort developed in Loren an ability to persist in the face of adversity. It also created in him a deep thirst for approval that had to be ministered to in later years.

During her preschool years in Streator, Illinois, Ami, our second child, was the only little girl on the block. Sometimes she was allowed to tag along with Loren and his friends but never as a full-fledged member of the group. She felt this exclusion keenly and responded to it in several ways, including: (1) She assumed what she felt was the upper hand by becoming more righteous than her older brother, reminding him quietly but persistently about the rewards of virtuous living. This practice did nothing to win her a place in the group, but it did give her an identity in relation to them. (2) She became a pint-sized champion of the underdog, her heart bleeding for anyone who was underprivileged, taunted, or teased. She'd take them under her wing, no matter what the cost, and mother them.

In one community where we lived there was a very poor family named "Pitts." The children's parents took good care of them, and they were respectable in every way. But they dressed in clothing that was ill-fitting, and they bore the marks of an inadequate diet. Neighborhood children took up the cruel taunt, "Pitts, Pitts—you look like the pits," and they passed a warning to newcomers, "Be careful—you'll catch the Pitts!"

Ami identified and became one with the rejected, defending them faithfully. We admired her for the love and strength she demonstrated. We worried a little for fear of feeding her self-righteous stance. We worried more for the pattern of mothering that was so much a part of her. When she married, the Lord blessed the mothering as she applied it to her children. But He had to purge and refine the mothering insofar as it was for a time inappropriately and unconsciously applied to her husband. It was not enough to make the grown Ami aware mentally of what she was doing. The little girl inside had to be comforted, forgiven, and released from the driving urgency in her heart. Then she could choose to relate freely to Ron in a love that nurtured him according to his need.

TEASING

Even when teasing is intended not as ridicule but as an affectionate expression, it can be damaging to preschool children. They do not understand teasing, tending to interpret what is said very literally. Most of us have experienced the tearful response of a little child who has just been told, "The cat has your tongue," or "I have your nose," followed by a tweak of said appendage (with the thumb thrust between second and third fingers to prove it). Or the loud response to, "You have epidermis all over you!"— "I do not!" Many of us have not realized the wounding we have inflicted by continual use of expressions such as: "Hi, twerp!" "How'd you grow so short?" "Come on, dummy." "Hey, stupid." We adults may think we are communicating such epithets as jokes by our laughter, but the heart of the child receives it as ridicule and rejection. He feels attacked unjustly for his size or his ignorance, over which he has no control.

Perhaps the most common thing we pray for to enable a person to live beyond feelings of being inadequate or unacceptable in (or home) his adult peer group is in relation to teasing by other children years ago. The adult mind can remember and identify the occasion and the confusion. The person needs to recall that place and time in his heart, forgive those who teased him, be forgiven for his anger and possible continual, habitual lashing out or with-drawal from others, and accept a renewed identity.

RIDICULE

A child who is ridiculed in front of his classmates may carry the scars of the knife thrust for years. He may carry anxiety within his heart about embarrassing himself in front of other people. A child who wets his pants in class and is pointed out as a baby who can't control himself may from then on harbor feelings of embarrassment and rejection about his body and its natural functions. He may carry hate in his heart toward the teacher who would not recognize his need to leave the room. He can then project that hatred on anyone who ignores his desires or puts him on the spot for whatever reason. But the good news is that today he can also by his choice describe that hurtful incident to the Lord and let someone pray in order that forgiveness may be accomplished. He can pray that the power of that incident to push or inhibit him be broken. Jesus will answer that prayer.

As a child I (Paula) was very performance oriented, so much so that when I was fitted for new glasses, I faked the ability to read the print in a storybook (I had memorized the story by repeated listening) because I thought new glasses meant I was *supposed* to see clearly. I couldn't let anyone know I was failing to do what I was supposed to be able to do. I can laugh about that now, but it was a very serious matter to the little girl. I carried my "ought world" into the classroom, mixed with a good measure of shyness. Although I can't remember the names of the teachers who were sensitive and considerate, that part of my heart is at peace.

At age six I made a powerful, hateful secret judgment against a teacher who called me "stupid" because I would not follow her directions about spelling my name. I quietly persisted in writing "Paula" on the blackboard while she accelerated to a public display of temper at my expense because I didn't know how to write my name "correctly" as "Pauline." Later she sent me on an errand that I blundered because I didn't hear her clearly, and she scathed me publicly for being "stupid." I remember her name because it was written in blood in my heart and fed with resentment.

For years I was hypersensitive to remarks that were made thoughtlessly perhaps but innocently, which I received as insults. Having judged her for calling me stupid, I found myself reaping that judgment by putting others down. They felt "stupid" though I never called them that. I have since come into a deep dimension of freedom from that bondage. Jesus cannot free us from hatred and resentment when we think we have a right to hate and resent.

FAMILY POSITION AND OTHER ASSORTED OPPORTUNITIES TO FOUL

We may be loved, taught, and nurtured marvelously and yet be imperfect and erring. For example, an only child may have striving in him because he was always running on tiptoe to live up to an adult model. He may be self-centered because in the home he was always the center of attention. He may find it difficult to share his space because he never had to. He may not know the freedom of good-natured rough-and-tumble with others because he never knew how to rough-and-tumble with brothers and sisters who would come up laughing after rolling and pounding on the floor.

If we were last children, we may always feel tacked on, a tagalong in relationships, or that we never quite measure up to others' abilities. If we were first children, we may be too dutiful and serious or have a habit of fleeing from responsibility, having been given too much too soon. We may feel controlled and pushed because we were that first project for parents who were practicing on us. Middle children may flounder, not knowing whether they belong with the older kids or the younger.

If our family is talented, we may have trouble coming up with something that is only ours to do and feel like we can't measure up to our siblings. If our family has no talent, we may feel like nothing can sparkle coming from a setting like that. If our home was always neat, we may be unable to tolerate disorder. If we lived in disorder, we may feel guilt and helplessness deep inside about that, especially if as children we heard apologies again and again for "messes the children make."

All of us are filled with memories of little things we made into big deals. Everyone in my second grade wore short socks while I had to wear knee socks, so I rolled my knee socks down to be like everyone else. Our son Tim didn't feel handsome in glasses, so he managed to "lose" multiple pairs. Perhaps our jeans didn't have the "right" kind of pockets. It may be that the way people related to our differentness was by wounding. All such things may leave hidden trigger points inside us or not-so-hidden harmful practices. But in Jesus we are healed simply by inviting Him to minister to that place in our hearts that still harbors those childhood hurts and to bring resultant practices to death on the cross. From then on, no one can force us to pick our scabs.

ABUSED

If we were abused physically or emotionally as children, we may have foundation stones of fear, rejection, anger, and a thousand variations. We will need to have basic trust restored in us before we can reach out with confidence to Father God or to any authority figure. If a prayer minister ministers in the nature of Jesus by the wisdom and power of Jesus, tuned in to His direction so as not to rape the process, always aiming sensitively to connect the person to Jesus, there is no wound beyond healing, no experience beyond redemption. The inner heart needs to be ministered to, and the solely effective method is the cross.

> I pray that the *eyes of your heart may be enlightened,* so that you may know what is the hope of His calling, what are the riches of the glory of His inheritance in the saints, and what is the surpassing greatness of His power toward us who believe. These are in accordance with the working of the strength of *His* might.
> —EPHESIANS 1:18–19, EMPHASIS ADDED

We cannot enter the narrow gate into the fullness of life in the kingdom carrying a load of garbage. Having examined that which is in our hearts to determine what is garbage, we must leave it at the altar of God and go on. If we do not do that, we cannot go on to freedom and maturity.

I (Paula) was a first child. My parents were almost as inexperienced at being parents as I was a novice at learning what it is to be a child of God. We blessed one another. We made mistakes. We sinned against one another in our ignorance and immaturity and because of our basic sinful tendencies. But in Jesus we are forgiven and forgiving, transformed and renewed. I have needed to see the shape of me, to dig to the foundation stones to let Jesus happen in me. Now, as the adult child of my parents, leaving the hurtful part of the past behind, I can grow forward with the cherished remembered heritage of the wealth of my parents to strengthen, encourage, and instruct my life.

> Observe the commandment of your father, and do not forsake the teaching of your mother; bind them continually on your heart; tie them around your neck. When you walk about, they will guide you; when you sleep, they will watch over you. And when you awake, they will talk to you.
> —PROVERBS 6:20–22

It is important not only to heal the wounds of childhood, but also to honor and cherish the good memories. Honoring and remembering build strength into us to stand. My advice: cherish your own upbringing in every way that was good.

OUT OF THE CHOSEN TREASURE OF MY HEART I REMEMBER DAD

Skating hand in hand
When I was two—
The left skate on him.
The right on me,
And feeling together.

His calling me "Baby,"
But never
Making me feel like one.
"You can do anything
you really want to do."

His pretending to "only look"
In our mouths
For loose teeth—
And coming up grinning
With quick and painless extractions.

His coming home after
Days of travel on the road
To take us for a ride in the car—
Buying special treats.
We each could choose
When wonderfully delicious things
Could be bought for a nickel,
And nickels were hard to come by.

Sitting on the piano bench
Announcing his homecoming
With *chiri-biri-bin* on the clarinet—
A special quality of order
Settling over the household
With the music of his presence.
Rocking the little ones
To the only songs he ever sang—
"The Old Gray Mare"
and "Bye O Baby Bunting."

His grossing mother out
With ridiculous humor
When life became too serious and cares too heavy—
Teaching us to laugh at ourselves.
A legacy our boys have inherited.

I remember him
Buried under piles of weekend job reports,
Pecking away at his typewriter—
Taking time from that important task
To let his dentures slip out the corner of his mouth
For our amusement.

His creative cookery—that special sauce for pork and beans
His books—tomato plants—his picture taking
His "dag-nab-it" when things went wrong.
(I never heard him swear.)

He could show tender emotions
And yet
Stand sturdy in the face of our anxiety and say
"It will be all right"
With believable authority we could touch.

He could charm the proverbial "face off a clock"
Without departing from the truth,
Plug away at life without being dreary,
Lay down his life without putting any under obligation,
And win a prize for being human,
Without expecting a medal.
He even cried with the rest of us when our kitty died.

Every special day—
Birthday,
Christmas
Father's Day—
It was the same.
I spent my dime,
My two weeks' fortune saved
For a gift for Dad:
White wrapped,
Ribbon curled,
Small and flat—
Always the same, and ever a surprise
To Him.
He'd smile and effervesce,
"Well, look here what it is!"
And proudly wear
My love
And me
In his pocket.

I REMEMBER MOM

Rocking, singing
Sharing her repertoire
Of a hundred nursery rhymes to give her children.

Loving us through
Bumps and mumps and whoops and sniffles
With milk toast, clean white sheets,
And sometimes purple plaster on our chests
Under soft flannel—
Such fun to peel off in the morning.

I remember
The delightful smells from the kitchen—
Chicken pot pie
Meat loaf
Grape jam simmering
Peanut butter cookies
Green beans with bacon and onion
And we always sat together at the table
With a prayer of praise to the Provider.

She played the piano while we sang
For hours.
If we were scattered in a thousand alluring directions,
We were reunited in a foundation of the
Great old songs of Christian faith.
And they remained,
And we were stayed.

I remember her presence at every school function.
We knew her interest,
And we understood authority;
"If you're spanked at school, you'll be
spanked again at home."
And our house was not divided against itself.
It stands.

She could iron her way through
Baskets of freshly laundered clothes
And tromp with us
On aching legs
To the zoo—or through an art museum.
Her answer to rambunctious
Troops of neighborhood boys
Was an afternoon trip to a packing plant or jam factory.
In our family
We were free to be rotten
But not to get by with it.
The discipline was pruning—never excommunication.

Sunday
Was always the first day of the week in our home
From the beginning.
And it was Sabbath:
Sunday school and worship,
Family dinner and rest,
Funny papers and games,
Music through a long afternoon.
Edgar Bergen and Charlie McCarthy and "One Man's Family"
In the evening
With the aroma of toasted cheese, peanut butter,
And sassafras tea.
Life and God all flowed together.
(Sunday evening still smells like that
whether the sandwiches are there or not.
And if the Lord's Day is given away,
The month is one long dreary week.)

Charlie and Edgar have passed away
But the family goes on
And multiplies in blessing...

Renewed each day by life from roots
That never die.

Hot summer sun and
Row on row of bright clean clothes
Flapping on the lines.
Mother:
Stooping,
Stretching,
Folding,
Carrying,
While we played in the yard and vacant lot—
Exploring trails,
Weaving clover chains,
And capturing grasshoppers
For our Mason-jar zoo.

Some plan and scheme and push as children grow
And bind their offspring to them as they go
In selfish striving.
But Mother launched her dreams from ironing boards,
And blessed their rising.

CHAPTER 6

BREAKING CHILDHOOD INNER VOWS

Again, you have heard that the ancients were told, "You shall not make false vows, but shall fulfill your vows to the Lord." But I say to you, make no oath at all, either by heaven, for it is the throne of God, or by the earth, for it is the footstool of His feet, or by Jerusalem, for it is the city of the great King. Nor shall you make an oath by your head, for you cannot make one hair white or black. But let your statement be, "Yes, yes" or "No, no"; and anything beyond these is of evil.

—MATTHEW 5:33–37

A woman came to us who could not bear a male child. Several times she had become pregnant and had miscarried boys about the third or fourth month. Gynecologists could find no physical cause. She fervently wanted to give her husband a son. We asked about her life with her father and could find some hurts, but her reactions did not seem great enough to create such a destructive, obviously psychosomatic condition. Her brother, however, was not like the usual sibling who teases because he loves. This brother was vicious, continually embarrassing and physically hurting her. Her father failed to protect her. She remembered then, at nine or ten, walking beside a river, picking up stones, hurling them into the water, crying out, "I'll never carry a boy child. I'll never carry a boy child." That was an inner vow, a directive sent through the heart and mind to the body. Though the conscious mind had long forgotten, the inner being had not. Though she now wanted to give birth, the earlier programming was still intact and functioning.

We took up authority in Christ, knowing that whatever we loose on the earth is loosed in heaven (Matt. 16:19; 18:18). Having pronounced forgiveness for her hatred of her brother and induced her to forgive, we spoke directly to her body, even as Jesus rebuked the fever (Luke 4:39). We commanded the body to forget that hateful order and to return to the original command of God, to "be fruitful and multiply, and fill the earth, and subdue it" (Gen. 1:28). Mentioning "subdue" was a polite way of reminding the body, as part of nature, to obey the voice of the Lord even as Jesus commanded the waves and the winds and they obeyed Him (Matt. 8:23–27). We prayed comfort and healing for her heart, spirit, and body. In the prayer, the Lord caused us to see her being able to produce a healthy, normal baby boy. She did conceive and carried to full term a normal healthy son.

An inner vow is a determination set by the mind and heart into all the being, usually in early life. It is a key element in the "fortress" we build in our heart to protect us from pain. Second Corinthians 10:4–5 says:

> For the weapons of our warfare are not of the flesh, but divinely powerful for the destruction of fortresses. We are destroying speculations and every lofty thing raised up against the knowledge of God, and we are taking every thought captive to the obedience of Christ.

In Greek, the word here for "thought" is *noema*. This is not just any passing thought. *Noema* means "a purpose" or "device of the mind."[1] An inner vow is a type of *noema*, a permanent "device of the mind." It is a promise one makes to himself, usually with the words *never* or *always*, to do something to permanently stop or prevent pain: "I will hurt people before they can hurt me" (so I won't have to feel so powerless). "I will always be perfect" (so no one will find reason to criticize me). "I will never open my heart again" (so no one can hurt me). "I will never trust anyone" (so no one can betray me). These are some of the building blocks of the self-protective fortresses in our hearts. Unfortunately, such fortresses fail to keep away pain. But they do keep away the blessings they "guard" until we agree to let Him tear them down. For He will have us rely on no defense but the spiritual armor He supplies (Eph. 6:13–17).

Vows we make currently also affect us, but an *inner* vow is usually one set into us as children, usually forgotten. Our inner being persistently retains such programming no matter what changes of mind and heart may later pertain. The distinctive mark of an inner vow is that it resists the normal maturation process. "When I was a child, I used to speak as a child, think as a child, reason as a child; when I became a man, I did away with

135

childish things" (1 Cor. 13:11). We may have many childish pecu-
liarities, but we mature and leave them behind, reminded only
by friends, relatives, and family reminiscences. Normal childish
proclivities do not harm us other than to embarrass us as children, goading us to mature, until we "do away with them"; that is,
shyness, awkwardness, absentmindedness, insensitivity toward
others' feelings, and so on. But inner vows resist change. We do
not grow out of them.

Inner vows may not become manifest immediately in behavior.
Like the programming of a clock on an electric range, they may
not kick on until the time set by the vow. They may rest totally
forgotten and dormant until triggered by the right persons or
situations. Having forgotten them, we are unaware they exist or
could have any effect.

We have all made many inner vows of varying intensity and
tenacity. Inner vows are as common to children as peanut butter
in America. There are good and helpful vows as well as destructive ones. Even the good vows need to be released so that we are
not impelled by the flesh but by the Spirit in freedom. Vows do
need to be seen, for their nature is to prevent departure from
them. They affect us like a railroad track affects a train. The
conscious mind may be a very good engine, but it can run only
on the track the inner vow set for it in childhood. No matter
which way the engineer may desire to go, the train will not
change direction unless someone switches tracks. Inner vows,
being lodged in the heart like an engram,*respond not at all to

---

* An engram occurs when such a powerful trauma occurs that it produces an automatic reaction from then on. A scar is a good example of an emotional engram.
The wound on our skin faithfully produces that scarring mark. Just so, engrams
reproduce emotional reactions in our personality and character.

the fleshly will. Unaided, the person cannot uproot or change that track. Such vows require authority. Only one who knows his authority in the Lord Jesus Christ can break the power of a vow and reset the inner being to another way of acting.

Many marriages resemble a rail yard. Many tracks lead in. But too often the engine is not on the track leading to marital bliss. It runs on the track of hidden vows, far from happiness. Unless someone switches the track, the train to marital bliss will never arrive. Though perhaps a person alone, with Jesus, could reset his own tracks, he should prefer not to. It is much easier, humbler, and better to let another in the body of Christ do it with us. Pride is best humbled by the body of Christ ministering to us.

Another young wife who could not conceive came to us. She greatly wanted to bear children for her husband. According to her gynecologist, tests revealed no physical reasons for barrenness either in her or her husband. She should normally have conceived easily long before. Questioning revealed that she had been the eldest of nine children born to a Catholic woman who became ill early in each pregnancy and remained so until long after delivery.

It took little imagination to see what happened each time her mother conceived. Feelings of imposition increased yearly, as she had to take over and run the household. Anger mounted day by day, pregnancy after pregnancy, at her mother for continuing to become pregnant, at her father for causing it, at the church for its rules, and at all the babies who caused commotion and labor. Ultimately she cried out over and over again, "I'll never be like my mother; I'll never act like that." Her inner being easily interpreted such vows as orders not ever to allow pregnancy.

Who can say how much power our determinations have to influence the functions of the body? Healthy, natural instincts and desires, even her love for her husband, could not overcome that earlier directive.

I (John) pronounced forgiveness for her disrespect of her father and mother and the church, and by authority in the name of Jesus broke the power of that vow and directed her inner being and her body to receive and nurture life. She did conceive and bear a son; later a daughter was born. Would she have conceived in due time anyway? Or did her inner vow in fact prevent this from happening until the vow was broken? Who can say? We have seen this and similar inner vows broken so many times in prayer, with such immediate beneficial results, that to us the revelation is confirmed.

INNER VOWS MEN MAKE—IN RELATION TO MOTHERS

Many wives have discovered the trouble is that their husbands were raised by mothers! We don't mean that critically, however facetiously. Boys soon learn that mothers have elephantine memories. They discover that "whatever you say can and will be used against you in a court of law." Often, whatever emotion hangs out noticeably, good or bad, will be used by mama to control. So boys learn to hide from their mothers. The less she knows, the better. Whatever she knows may be hauled up for criticism or scolding—weeks, months, or years later. Though all this is normal, sometimes the situation is so tense or the reaction so vehement that the lad forms a most obstinate inner vow: "Never share what you really feel with a woman. It's not safe."

Later on, when chromosomes and hormones change a boy's

aversion to girls, he may want to share and find himself unable. Most likely he may find it easy to communicate with girls until he marries. Marriage puts the woman in position to trigger in him inner vows made relative to such primary females as mothers, grandmothers, and sisters. Frequently couples have come for prayer ministry, perplexed by the fact that they had good communication until the honeymoon. Now her complaint is: "He won't tell me anything anymore." Evening conversations sound something like the following:

"Hi, honey. How was your day?"

"Fine. Just fine."

"Tell me about it."

"What do you want to know?"

"How did it go? What happened today?"

"Just great. Went just great."

"Like what?"

"What, what?"

"You know, tell me some incidents. Tell me about your day."

"Oh, I don't know. Just like any other day I suppose."

"Well, what happened?"

"What do you mean, what happened?"

"Tell me some incidents. How did your day go?"

"I just told you, just like any other day. You know how the office goes."

In no way does he know that his inner being has no intention to share what is really on his heart. Unknown to him or her, earlier self-programming has kicked into action. Even if he hears his wife and is wounded and perplexed about his inability to be vulnerable to her, he may not be able to change his heart to open and share. He may repent a dozen times, only to return automatically to the pattern. The problem is that his repentances in the present concerning his wife cannot overcome the earlier directive of the vow concerning his mother. The repentance is true but for the wrong sin. It's like an arrow shot into the center of the bull's-eye—at the wrong target.

The repentance and prayer needed are for lingering childhood resentments toward his mother (and other primary females) and for the breaking of that inner vow he set into his being. Present surface repentances alone cannot touch such deeply set directives.

Such inner vows are among the most common problems men and women face. Many a husband, unaware perhaps that he isn't sharing, gradually becomes more and more estranged from his wife. Lacking him, she may be emotionally wilting and dying and may eventually find other places, like the church or bridge clubs, to find sharing and fulfillment. The husband meanwhile becomes lonelier and lonelier. Now he ripens for the almost inevitable affair. He has no way of knowing that if he divorces his wife and marries this woman who, "Thank God, understands me," the moment he marries her, she will then be in the identical "ruled out" position his wife presently occupies. That inner vow confines him to isolation from any wife who exposes him to vulnerability (limited but more than with his wife) to anyone who does not trigger the action of the vow. He is doomed to loneliness and possible superficial affairs until the vow is seen and broken.

Unlike the two former examples, merely seeing and breaking the inner vow will not by itself set him free. In the former two, I (John) could speak to the body, which was eagerly willing to return to the original command of God to produce life. The body

140

leaped, unimpeded, to fulfill its purpose in creation. Few structures in the soul remained to block. But in the case of vows not to share, many other character structures remain after the original inner vow is broken.

Those who have seen the movie *Star Trek: The Motion Picture* know that when Voyager VI returned, a planet of machines had built a vast complex subplanet of mechanisms around the original small probe—that was still seeking to fulfill its original mission! Just so, inner vows of this type have built huge surrounding complexes in the character structure, and all are still seeking to fulfill that original purpose—to hide the person from hurt. There may be, for example, a heart of stone; unconscious, evasive, and defensive habitual flight mechanisms; automatically triggered angers; many bitter-root expectancies; or key words, phrases, or actions that stimulate automatic reactions, deep anxieties and fears, incapability to trust, and so on. After all these negatives are overcome, there will still exist the need to create totally new habit structures to replace the old. Extended prayer ministry may be required, as one by one all the auxiliary structures are dismantled or transformed. Patience by all—wife, husband, and prayer minister—will be necessary, plus forbearance, compassion, and continuous forgiveness. It may take a long time to overcome the many complex "machines" of one little vow.

INNER VOWS WOMEN MAKE

In a woman, the most common malformation she encounters is likewise an inability to share who she is with the man of her life—not usually, however, in the area of talking. On the surface, in communication, women almost invariably are more desirous of sharing than men are, so much so that sometimes that fact itself is part of the problem: "Your desire shall be for your husband!" (Gen. 3:16). Eve's desire was already by creation for Adam. The Lord meant that her desire would become inordinate, made so by insecurity. "A sandy ascent for the feet of the aged—such is a garrulous wife to a quiet husband" (Ecclesiasticus 25:20, Apocrypha, NRSV). God created the woman to desire to please her husband, but right there is the entrance to trouble, for women were likewise raised with their fathers.

Little girls want to be the apple of their daddies' eyes. They come to Earth innately knowing they are God's gift to ravish their daddies' hearts, to comfort, delight, and please. Being received by an appreciative father builds confidence in what it is to be a woman. A wife fulfills her husband from her own sense of beauty and desirability. If she knows she is a precious gift of God to him, his life with her will be restful and blessed. If she doesn't and therefore requires constant stated approval and reaffirmation, she becomes a wearisome burden to her man. He always has to prove to her anew that she is desirable to him. That wears him out. He becomes vulnerable to some "siren" who seems "confident" of her desirability.

Unfortunately, not enough fathers are aware of their value. Even fewer are dead enough to self-centeredness to be aware for their girls' sakes rather than their own. Too many times little girls have bounded joyfully into their daddy's presence, only to be ignored or pushed away. New dresses were not noticed, or dad only said, "Yeah, it's OK," or to mama, "What did it cost?" School papers may not have been rewarded with compliments. Worse, the little girl, who lived from a romantically emotional world her father had long since forgotten, may have seen mother's heart crushed again and again mostly by what daddy failed to notice. Men, to her, eventually became regarded as "dumb," "off base," not noticing or knowing where life really is.

For this reason, God in His Word almost never has to remind the woman to love the man; she would have already. But "let the wife see to it that she *respect* her husband" (Eph. 5:33, emphasis added). "Thus Sarah obeyed Abraham, calling him lord, and you have become her children if you do what is right without being frightened by any fear" (1 Pet. 3:6). The "fear" is not usually of physical abuse but of anxiety born of distrust—"The man will not see and do what will make me feel secure."

From constantly repeated neglects and slights, a little girl originates a subtle inner vow. A man's childish vow is not as subtle. It's simply, "Don't share." But a woman retains a hunger to meet and fulfill her man. Hidden to the grown one, the most common forgotten inner vow of little girls has been, "Don't let him really have or know all of you." Sharing means from then on, first that the wife wants to share *his* life, to know *him* and talk about *him*, not the other way around. And second, her inner vow makes a clever game of what she does share with her husband. She may share enough of herself and give enough to him to convince herself that she is the open and sharing one, unaware that she has unconsciously and carefully controlled how much she is sharing. He does not really have all of her, in the very moments of sharing in which her surface life protests otherwise.

How often have little girls clenched their fists in frustration when daddy didn't notice them? How often have daddy's words revealed he never really understood her at all? From reactions to such experiences grow distrust and disrespect, which strengthen the inner vow not to be vulnerable, not to really risk who she is with a man. "See if I ever..." As in a boy, by the time natural desire reverses childhood aversion, the earlier directives are not only forgotten, but also often they would be vehemently denied.

But that inner vow is only the tip of the iceberg. Statistics show that one out of every three to four girls has been sexually assaulted by the age of eighteen.[2] When little girls broadcast their desire to be seen and held, many men receive the signals but interpret them sexually. They fail to honor the call to be fathers and honorable men who can love a girl to life as a desirable woman. They respond sexually and thus violate not only the girl's body but also her precious ability to trust herself to openly be her own lovely person with the right man. From the moment of molestation she may fear to let the beauty of who she is shine for fear the result will be nastiness. A most passionate inner vow screams through her being—"Shut down!"

From then on, she may become either frigid or promiscuous; behind both is the same cause, an inability to give herself fully to the man of her life. She may appear sexy and have intercourse often, righteously (that is, within marriage) or unrighteously. She may enjoy sex or detest it, but behind all this, there is a covert inability to be all she is to the man. She cannot meet her man unreservedly with all her heart and spirit through her body. Sex is confined to physical stimulation, because her spirit is not free to flow out and nestle into her man. Her man may find himself bemused, confused by something intangible he senses is lacking. He cannot understand why, with a willing wife (if that is her case), he still hungers for others. The truth is that he has never yet had her. Loneliness is most poignant when there seems to be no reason for it.

Renouncing Inner Vows

It may be difficult at first to see the problem inner vows create. All apparent clues may indicate that she gives while the husband doesn't and that he can't or won't receive her. Lack of clarity may be compounded by the fact that in truth he can't open or receive, both in communication and in their sex life. We have found it a wise principle that problems in marriages are never one-sided. Whatever problem appears in one mate, in the other there is something either counterbalancing or identical, usually equally disturbing or destructive. This is especially important to remember when we see a beautiful saintly woman with a callous, uncouth man.

Our first task in getting free from the power of inner vows is to get help from a trusted prayer minister. Once we see the inner vow at work, we can come to a real hatred, not of any person or thing outside ourselves, but of that practice in our character that blocks us from real life. We must come to hatred of the inner vow that caused the blocking practice. Such hatred is not automatic and should not be taken for granted. Fruits, not words, reveal truth. It takes time before fruits are steadfastly manifest. Prayer should be immediate for the dishonoring of parents to be forgiven, for the vows to be broken, and for the new life of freedom to emerge, but it may take a while before there is proper hatred of the old ways and consequent death of self.

Again, the fullness of transformation cannot be achieved without resurrection. A woman whose father never loved her to life may come to know herself outwardly as beautiful and desirable, and even flaunt it, while inwardly feeling ugly and undesirable. A truly confident person does not need to flaunt, preen, or brag. Flirting, or any hint of making use of sexual allurement, is usually a dead giveaway to inner arid deserts and distress. No matter how many things come to death on the cross, lasting results cannot happen without resurrection. Resurrection is enabled only by love. A person cannot come to life without being loved to life (1 John 4:19). The little girl needs a father.

Paula and I have acted as father and mother in Christ to many such women. But all too many times we have seen ministers and counselors caught in transferences and being seduced. We warn every prayer minister stringently to keep the cross between himself and the person to whom he ministers, to guard his own heart and feelings carefully, to be secure in his own mate (or in the watchful counsel of others if unmarried), to be securely girded in the moral law of God's Word, and to be regularly in devotion and worship. The attempt to love the other to life must be kept by the prayer minister, not by the person receiving ministry. Prayer ministers must know themselves to be fathers and mothers in Christ—and nothing else.

Fruits are not hard to detect. They cannot be hidden. "You are the light of the world. A *city set on a hill cannot be hidden*" (Matt. 5:14, emphasis added). Whatever degree of physical glamour a woman may naturally possess, when she also becomes beautiful from within, nothing can hide it. Beauty suffuses from inside and settles about her without attracting wrong attention. Men treat her as the lady she has become. Quiet inner joy now radiates, no matter whether for the moment she is sad or happy. She is free to give to her husband without demanding tit-for-tat reciprocation. Because he is free from demand, he usually begins to respond.

One lady reported with delight, "He can't keep his hands off me. He's always patting me and telling me how he loves me." Because she has become free, many talents long bound begin to be discovered and soon flower. Prayer ministers need to stand back and let it happen.

VARIOUS KINDS OF VOWS

Inner vows are as multifarious as people are. Some are simple, like a boy who swears he will never sing (because of early embarrassments or a demanding parent), only years later to discover a rich voice being released through prayer ministry. Some are complex, like a girl who refuses to put her head under water when swimming, but through prayer ministry she discovers it has nothing to do with early swimming experiences and everything to do with a vow never to be risked beyond her control. In Paula's case, that vow had started in the water of the womb and had been strengthened by demands to perform beyond her age level. Only now, years after the infilling of the Holy Spirit and more years of seeing and praying over root causes, is she beginning to be free in the water!

People can make vows never to speak in public, never to develop breasts, never to grow up, never to give of self or even of simple things like clothes, never to allow personal space to be invaded, or never to wear hand-me-downs. Many inner vows have to do with ambitions—"I'll be the best ever," "I'll never fail again," or their opposite, "I'll never try again."

The most vitiating are those concerning personal relationships. Children can make other powerful determinations against parents, as we discussed earlier, that destroy marital relationships.

The inner vow "I'll get even with her" (mother or sister) can lead to an unconscious need to take vengeance on all women, specifically on one's wife and children.

The inner vow "I'll never let him (brother or sister) get the best of me again" (in reaction to either teasing or sibling rivalry) can result in automatic hidden competitive and/or evasive mechanisms with a spouse and close friends.

Some inner vows set a person upon untenable courses that lead to breakdowns or explosions. "I'll never let my temper go again; see what resulted when I did?" Thereafter such a person may store up repressed anger until the mere spark sets off a holocaust.

"Never again will I be unprepared when people ask me a question." Such a person may be tense in every group until he has figured out how to respond to every possible question. When he is put into too many situations involving too many quick adjustments, his inner vow becomes a major contributing factor to a breakdown.

Good inner vows need to be renounced lest they block normal healthy interchanges. I (John) turned many of my parents' good teachings into strong inner vows: "Never hit a woman." "Never raise your voice to a woman." "Keep your temper." "Treat every woman as a lady." Such vows are good, but when they cause us to depend on the strength of our own willpower rather than on the gracious provision of the Holy Spirit, they are of the flesh and binding, not of the spirit of freedom. Those inner vows and others of their ilk made me unreal with Paula. Rejecting them did not release a boomerang to violence. Never yet have I hit Paula or tried to wound by insulting, and the fact that I am free to lose my temper and raise my voice has never resulted in my becoming a loud or angry person.

And I am probably even less likely to become so for the fact that the Lord, rather than my fleshly determination, controls me in those areas. If not released to the Lord, my vows would have locked me into reactions that later would have had to find some form of outlet. Perhaps more importantly, our righteousness must become His by the flow of His Holy Spirit in us, not by the strivings and consequent pride of fleshly determinations.

WHEN TO SUSPECT INNER VOWS

With the help of a prayer minister, we should look for inner vows behind stubborn practices in our character. Compulsive behavior may (or may not) indicate inner vows at their root; other factors may be at work. In each case we must discern whether a vow is in fact at the root of our trouble. Where inner vows do lie at the root, seldom are they the sole factor. They work in tandem with bitter roots, hidden resentments and fears, and so on. But if not the sole factor, they are often the key factor. If there is a continuing lack of change, most specifically when other roots and practices have already been discerned and repentance should already have accomplished freedom, inner vows ought to be suspected and ferreted out.

Again, power (*dunamis*) such as would be needed to heal the physical body is not needed, but only the power (*exousia*) of authority. The least Christian who understands his authority (*exousia*) in Christ can break any inner vow. The prayer should not be merely hortatory, not "Lord, give him strength to over-come this inner vow," or petitionary, "Please take away this inner vow, dear Lord." Such prayer will accomplish little if anything. The situation requires prayer in first-person authority: "In Jesus's name, I break this inner vow." It cannot be effective when said as a magic ritual by one who does not truly know the Lord or believe his own authority in the Lord. We must have faith in the power and will of the Lord to act.

A simple prayer will suffice. But it doesn't hurt to express it several ways so the heart can fully grasp it. A sample prayer might be:

> *In Jesus's name I break the power of this inner vow to withdraw. I speak directly to the heart and say in Jesus's name, I release you from this habit of withdrawal, and I restore you to the original delight of your soul to share you with your brothers and sisters in Christ. I release you to open your heart and be* with *others. Thank You, Jesus, I see [name of person] talking and laughing, no longer afraid to make a mistake, giggling in freedom rather than embarrassment. I praise You, Lord, that You will continue until [the person's name] is one day able to say with an exclamation of joy, "Hey, it's true. I'm free, even as we prayed that day." Thank You, Jesus. Amen.*

If no one is available to pray with you, understand that this same prayer can be said by any person by himself, for himself. But whenever possible, pray with others, for reasons I previously expressed.

CHAPTER 7

A HEART OF STONE FOR A HEART OF FLESH

> Moreover, I will give you a new heart and put a new spirit within you; and I will remove the heart of stone from your flesh, and give you a heart of flesh.
>
> —EZEKIEL 36:26

> Do not harden your hearts, as in Meribah, as in the day of Massah in the wilderness; when your fathers tested Me, they tried Me, though they had seen My work. For forty years I loathed that generation, and said they are a people who err in their heart, and they do not know My ways. Therefore I swore in My anger, truly they shall not enter into my rest.
>
> —PSALM 95:8–11

God wants to raise a people with whom He can have fellowship, "that you also may have fellowship with us; and indeed our fellowship is with the Father, and with His Son Jesus Christ" (1 John 1:3)—He has saved us for Himself. It is not so much that He wants servants as that He hungers for friends (John 15:15). "And the Scripture was fulfilled which says, 'And Abraham believed God, and it was reckoned to him as righteousness,' *and he was called the friend of God*" (James 2:23, emphasis added). "Jesus answered and said to him, 'If anyone loves Me, he will keep My word; and My Father will love him, and We will come to him, and *make Our abode with him*'" (John 14:23, emphasis added).

To have fellowship with God requires capacity within our spirits to commune with Him. "God is spirit, and those who worship Him must worship in spirit and truth" (John 4:24). In human conversations almost all of us have experienced those rare moments when communion of spirit enabled us to so read each other's hearts that we seemed to comprehend before words were spoken. At other times, our words have appeared to bounce off invisible walls. We know then that we have spoken *at* each other but not *with* each other. Real fellowship is dependent upon the ability of our spirits to reach out and deeply connect with one another.

We can understand and be refreshed in one another's company only if our spirits are able to meet and nourish one another. Anyone who has touched the clamminess of a corpse has recognized the absence of spirit. A "dead fish" handshake is defined by that fact—lack of meeting and embracing. How often have we spent hours with someone, only to realize "I never really met him," or in a moment's embrace felt like we had always known as a friend someone we just met?

Men can understand men because each possesses a man's spirit. Similarly, all creation seeks its own, cats with cats, dogs with dogs, and so on. No cow ever mistakes a horse for a cow because a cow knows its own kind.

By design, each species communes with its own. But God has created us human, and yet He desires to have fellowship with us! In the beginning, He made us able, breathing life into us by His own Spirit (Gen. 2:7). Adam and Eve walked and talked with Him in the Garden of Eden (Gen. 3:8). But in the Fall mankind mostly lost that capacity. We died in sin. Our attempts to commune with God became like a machine wired for one hundred volts trying to plug into a billion. No wonder the Israelites cried out, "Speak to us yourself [Moses] and we will listen; but let not God speak to us, lest we die" (Exod. 20:19).

So God came in human flesh, in Jesus, that through Him we might be restored to fellowship. Our Lord Jesus Christ poured out the Holy Spirit upon us so that we might have within us again the power to comprehend Him and His love (1 Cor. 2:14; Eph. 3:18–19), to commune and walk with Him in spirit (Rom. 8:14–16).

The difficulty is that the Holy Spirit comes to reside inside the barbed wire of our still-too-inhuman character. The Spirit, like water, must flow out through the shape of what we are. And God's approaches to us have to be interpreted by our still-imperfect, corrupted mentality. The union of the Holy Spirit with our *spirit* may be full and true, but meanings can become twisted altogether by the *heart* and *mind.* For example, if He comes to embrace us because of His love and compassion in spite of our waywardness, we can and often do take that moment of glory in His presence as confirmation that our wrong way is not only right but also His will for us.

It follows, then, that the more our hearts are open to Him and the more our minds comprehend, the better our fellowship.

Conversely, the harder and more stubborn our hearts are and the less our minds are akin to His, the less our ability to abide in fellowship. If our spirits meet His, understanding must match or we cannot sustain. That is one reason why Jesus said, "... in spirit *and truth*" (John 4:24, emphasis added). Spirit to spirit without truth causes a relationship to flow like a bankless river in the desert—soon gone! Truth alone is only mind to mind—and barren! Neither without the other can produce or sustain fellowship. Both spirit and truth together spark and enhance in crescendo to blessedness.

In the beginning, our marriage to the Lord overflows all our barriers, like a flood spilling over a dam. But we are still too carnal, too immature in faith to maintain that fullness of relationship. Soon the flow is behind the dam again, and we wonder where the Lord went. He is right there of course, but we can't sustain full fellowship due to our hardness of heart and lack of faith. Truth didn't match spirit; we couldn't abide.

The same happens in human relationships. At times our spirits leap over all barriers and we enjoy enriching fellowship. At other times we live in pockets of loneliness.

In order to enable true fellowship between humans and with Himself, God has to pierce or melt our hearts of stone so that His Spirit and ours can flow *through* to one another rather than only occasionally *over next* to one another. In our fallen condition, we are like medieval knights in armor, peering out slits to slash and poke at one another, wishing that other fellow would open up so we could really meet him.

The problem is malformation of character, formed long before age six, but between six and twelve it is either overcome or cemented. The spirit that God breathed into us at creation (Gen. 2:7) found itself hampered, required to find expression through the corrupted soul of mankind's inherited carnality.

OPENING—OR CLOSING—TO LIFE

We are all equally subject to the sinful condition of mankind, but each person's spirit may also experience uniquely harmful factors. Parents may not want the pregnancy. Quarreling, tension, and too much violence may rend the atmosphere. By the time a person emerges from the womb, or shortly thereafter, his spirit's ability to trust and open to life may be greatly hindered or blocked altogether. "The wicked are estranged from the womb; these who speak lies go astray from birth" (Ps. 58:3). All of us are "the wicked"; "no one does right" (Ps. 14:1, 2; Rom. 3:10–12).

Even conscientious, well-intentioned mothers are frequently unable to interpret their baby's signals correctly. Baby is hungry, but mama changes his diaper. Or the child is not hungry—a pin sticks or diaper rash bothers, or voices have startled him, or maybe he just wants to have a good cry—but mother puts her breast in his mouth! Perhaps papa burps the infant with a rough hand when all he needed was a gentle rocking to sleep. Or brothers and sisters keep on pestering, making noises and funny faces, when all he wants is peace and quiet. Or, at 2:00 a.m. when baby wants to giggle and play, everybody else wants to sleep!

In the best of homes constant irritants are a normal part of a baby's life. What can he do with his emotions? With anger? Resentments? Loneliness? Fears? Longings? Need for solitude? He doesn't yet know the Lord so as to be able to forgive. The mind has not developed so as to reason. Self-control has not yet been built. There are no stopping places; he has to *be* stopped by touch and comforting, strength of daddy and warmth of mama, but often parents aren't there or they fail to understand. He just plain hurts when he hurts and revels when he revels.

Included along with such normal irritants, in some cases, are rejection, prolonged absences, and consequent unabated loneliness. Every baby knows and seeks his own daddy and mommy. As John the Baptist at six months in utero could recognize the presence of Jesus in Mary's womb (Luke 1:44), so every baby spiritually knows his own parents. But some are given up for adoption. Adults may understand that in some circumstances this is best, but to the baby it is nothing less than horrendous rejection.

A father may little realize his own value and fail to rock and play, hold and comfort, walk and talk in the long night hours. Mama may have been trained, in that most horribly wrong school, never to hold lest she spoil—four hours in the crib, feed, and four more in the crib. Or mama may decide not to nurse or be unable to do so. How can a baby handle such hurts? With what emotional tools?

In far too many instances, violence and terror are added. Some parents are cruel and insensitive. Red, shouting faces loom over the crib. Again and again, raving drunken voices shatter sleep. Hitting and screeching may break out at any moment. There are no dependabilities to rest in.

What can a baby do to protect himself? He hastens to build walls around his heart! He learns to check the impulse to let his spirit flow out unguarded to another. Gradually, but most surely, he forms a heart of stone. Babies in deplorable homes can hardly keep from forming strong turtle shells. Every person on the earth has fashioned such a hardened heart, some softer, some harder and thicker, depending usually upon the degree of pain suffered, but far more upon his reaction to that pain.

There are families who make it their ministry to receive foster babies from violent or broken homes. When the tiny babies arrive, they are rigid and tense, or jumpy, unable to let down into an embrace. Their eyes stare blankly. Usually after a few weeks of love and prayer, the babies become warm, cuddly, soft, and giggly. Their little spirits leap joyfully into the arms of whoever holds them.

But what of the many tragically wounded who are not healed by love?

To the degree that each of us has formed a heart of stone, we have to that degree failed to become fully human. To that same degree, we have closed down the very faculties needed for real interchange of heart and mind. We will not let the spirit be vulnerable, open to touch and embrace. It hurts too much. We hide behind stone walls. We are like the boy in Wordsworth's "Ode: Intimations of Immortality From Recollections of Early Childhood":

> Our birth is but a sleep and a forgetting:
> The Soul that rises with us, our life's Star,
> Hath had elsewhere its setting,
> And cometh from afar:
> Not in entire forgetfulness,
> And not in utter nakedness,
> But trailing clouds of glory do we come
> From God, who is our home:
> Heaven lies about us in our infancy!
> Shades of the prison house begin to close
> Upon the growing Boy,

But he beholds the light, and whence it flows,
He sees it in his joy;
The Youth, who daily farther from the east
Must travel, still is Nature's Priest,
And by the vision splendid
Is on his way attended;
At length the man perceives it die away,
And fade into the light of common day.[1]

Our spirits' faculties, shut up and imprisoned, wither and atrophy like unused muscles. We become like Sleeping Beauty or Snow White, asleep within while all our dwarfed talents weep without. It takes a Prince Charming (Jesus) to awaken our numbed spirit to life again. Or we become like the Tin Man on the road to Oz to get a heart, rusted to a stop, needing the oil of the Holy Spirit before we can walk the long yellow brick road to find a heart. That, by the way, is why such stories as *Snow White and the Seven Dwarfs* and *The Wizard of Oz* continue to live— they tell the truth about us, and something inside us is still alive enough to know it!

TRUE COMMUNION AND COMMUNICATION

Some people have talked all their lives and have never known a moment's communication. Some have never enjoyed true human fellowship, much less divine. Worse, such individuals may have little or no consciousness of their lack. They get along by surface, monkey-see-monkey-do "sharing," not only insensitive that their heart and spirit have not met the other but also ignorant that something else is available. They have become zombies walking through a luscious garden, wearing glasses that prevent them from seeing anything but dandelions.

Real conscience is cultivated solely by the ability of our spirit to love, to meet, to enter in and share another's life for the other's sake. That is why Jeremiah wrote, "Were they ashamed because of the abomination they have done? They were not even ashamed at all; they did not even know how to blush. Therefore they shall fall among those who fall" (Jer. 6:15). Their spirits were too nonfunctional to have enabled true conscience. That is one reason St. Paul also wrote, "Do you not know that God's kindness is meant to lead you to repentance?" (Rom. 2:4, RSV). It is God's kindness that so touches the heart with the kiss of life that the spirit revives, enabling the conscience to function; only then can repentance happen.

In "I-thou" encounters, each "I" meets and treats any other person as a revered "thou," spirit to spirit, heart to heart, mind to mind, openly and without impediment. I-thou can be pictured by imagining two sparks radiating light into and through each other until, if one is blue and the other yellow, a green field suffuses both equally without eradicating either, at once brightening both the original yellow and blue. Whoever learns to live in I-thou relationships learns to cherish the other. He hurts in anticipation of the other's hurt and therefore stops *before* a personal action might wound the other. This is the true function of conscience.

To the degree of hardness, imprisonment, or stubbornness in their hearts, people are unable to enter into I-thou relationships. Their encounters are thereby delimited to "I-it."[2] Attempts originate not purely from their "I" but also from their shell, reaching only meagerly the "thou" of the other, mainly only his shell. So the picture is of two much-diminished lights beneath nutshells, bouncing blue and yellow rays off one another mostly

159

unchanged. No green of mutuality appears, except in flicks of chance in the passing rays. Such people do not have functioning consciences, because to them no other has ever become a cherished "thou." Any other remains only an "it" to bounce off of, attack, or climb over.

COMING ALIVE IN JESUS

The tragedy of our culture is that men and women are becoming progressively less human. God wants to raise human beings. Jesus, who is patient and kind, gentle and compassionate, loving and forgiving, is the only truly human person. In Him, we are to become more and more human, more warm and loving, vulnerable, and compassionate.*

The task of fathers and mothers is to evoke humanity in their children from the beginning, to call forth the spirit to embrace, and then to build "truth"—the ability of heart and mind to interpret meanings and cherish others' intents. Thus, though each child must bear responsibility for the choices of his spirit, God holds parents accountable (Heb. 13:17), for they either enable or prevent "I-thou" encounters. Insofar as others can *introduce us to life, it is parents who give us the most potent opportunities to become human or inhuman!*

In the command, "Bring them up in the nurture and admonition of the Lord" (Eph. 6:4, KJV), it is those last words that tell. Only nurture *in the Lord* brings forth children who have learned how to contribute their "I" in love to another "thou" without overriding or being dominated themselves. Above all, parents

---

* We are not advocating "humanism," which is Satan's copy, in which man exalts himself, but our Lord's resurrection of mankind to His fullness in humanity.

are to help children to discover the secret of joy, that abundant life is found in laying down one's life in sacrificial service for every other "thou." We are to encourage children to become adults who persistently choose never to treat another "thou" as a usable, discardable, destructible "it"!

> But realize this, that in the last days difficult times will come. For men will be lovers of self, lovers of money, boastful, arrogant, revilers, disobedient to parents, ungrateful, unholy, unloving, irreconcilable, malicious gossips, without self-control, brutal, haters of good, treacherous, reckless, conceited, lovers of pleasure rather than lovers of God; *holding to a form of godliness, although they* have *denied its power;* and avoid such men as these.
>
> —2 TIMOTHY 3:1–5, EMPHASIS ADDED

That prophecy is increasingly fulfilled today primarily because fathers and mothers have failed to cherish. Hardened, inhuman hearts are the result. Consequently such persons have no true conscience. They cannot relate to the power of God, which is love, because they have never received it. Their spirits are dormant and incapable.

For that reason the curse of street gangs ravages city streets. Vandalism forces architects to build schools that look like prisons, without breakable windows. Parks must find indestructible toilet and sink fixtures. And crime rates soar. Repressed anger at parents must find outlets. The curse *is* beginning to come upon our land—"Behold, I am going to send you Elijah the prophet before the coming of the great and terrible day of the Lord. And he will restore the hearts of the fathers to their children, and the hearts of the children to their fathers, lest I come and smite the land with a curse" (Mal. 4:5–6).

Each sin listed in 2 Timothy 3:1–5 can happen only because the perpetrators cannot see and cherish any other "thou." I (John), being a normal person, would have to mentally subhumanize my brother to steal from him, or else the pain would be too great. The same goes for adultery, gossip, treachery, whatever.

In order to defraud Indians, Caucasian Americans dulled their consciences by calling Native Americans "savages," something less than human, objects to be gotten rid of—"the only good Injun is a dead 'un." African Americans had to be regarded as less than human by slave owners, or else they could not have reduced them to chattel in slavery. In those who have never known themselves as loved and cherished, no other can possibly be a "thou."

Lady Macbeth, desiring to do evil, cried out, "Come, you spirits / That tend on mortal thoughts, unsex me here, / And fill me from the crown to the toe top-full / Of direst cruelty! make thick my blood; / Stop up the access and passage to remorse, / That no compunctious visitings of nature, / Shake my fell purpose," lest her too human feeling prevent it.[3] But those listed in 2 Timothy 3 have no need to dehumanize themselves; they already have become dehumanized! Increasing crime rates are therefore nothing more or less than the mark of our defection from true parenthood in the Lord.

→| It is humanity that Satan desires to destroy.

→| It is the heart of stone that is Satan's tool to block humanity.

- It is parents whom God intended to call forth humanity in children to enable hearts of flesh to develop.

- It is parents who are to call forth a "thou" to life.

- It is parents who often force a child to build walls of stone.

- It is Jesus who became human to meet and melt hearts of stone, to give us hearts of flesh.

- It is a heart of flesh in Jesus that is God's gift to restore humanity.

- It is Jesus who makes us human.

Prayer ministers can help with this work and can see how and when a child reacted in pain to flee and hide. The task is to see the heart of stone and melt it in the fire of love. Though parents create the problem, a prayer minister can deal with the child's guilt for reacting. Therefore confession and forgiveness again are the access to the efficacy of the cross. But whereas authority can break an inner vow, and the blood can wash away guilt, and daily death of self on the cross brings a practice of the old nature to death on the cross, more is involved here than all these. For that reason Jesus came to "baptize you with the Holy Spirit *and fire*" (Matt. 3:11, emphasis added). Only the fire of love can melt a heart of stone.

In Hans Christian Andersen's fairy tale "The Snow Queen," Kay and Gerda were two friends who cared for each other as brother and sister, and they played happily in the fields. Along came the wicked Snow Queen one evening, who cast a dart of ice into Kay's heart, left him, but came back later and carried him away. Gerda went through great perils a long time searching for Kay. But when she finally found him, Kay was not happy to see her. He reviled and shouted at her and spat upon her. At last her love warmed him, the ice thorn slipped out, and Kay came to himself. Gerda and Kay played happily together in the fields again.[4]

Just so, companions and prayer ministers must search patiently to find the frozen hearts of their friends. But ironically, the most common sign of returning life is that the warmer the love given, the meaner the response. Fear of vulnerability creates hate. Each stony heart has a life of its own. It sings lies into the mind. "You know what happened before when you risked yourself." "You don't want to get hurt again." "It may be lonely this way, but at least it's safe." Some of those songs may be true. The lie is that it's better to be alone and dying. So the person we are trying to love to life strikes back.

Jesus said, "Blessed are you when men cast insults at you, and persecute you, and say all kinds of evil against you falsely, on account of Me. *Rejoice,* and be glad, *for your reward . . . is great*" (Matt. 5:11–12, emphasis added). Why rejoice? Our reward is that the other is coming to life! The life of the person is our joy, our reward. The sign of coming to life is pain, like when his leg has fallen asleep, and the first he is aware of it is when he feels a million pricking needles of pain—the reason is that the leg is coming to life again! But our loved one built that hiding place precisely to escape pain. Therefore the attack is automatic, to remove the menace before the walls crumble altogether. Rejoicing is part of praise and worship, which keeps the flow of Jesus's life pummeling the walls with torches of fire.

Who has not seen dating couples break apart, strangely enough because they drew so close that their hearts were becoming vulnerable? Husbands, more frequently than wives, often become meaner and meaner the more their wives express love. Just so, the transformation of hearts of stone is not accomplished by distant, safe prayers and well wishings. Hearts of stone can only be melted by persistent, pain-bearing hearts willing to lay themselves down daily, understanding and forgiving every time the quarry turns to attack, until the ice thorn melts. Precisely this kind of love is fire. "God is love" (1 John 4:8), and "our God is a consuming fire" (Heb. 12:29).

The love of God is made manifest in Jesus, whose walk of love on Earth culminated in crucifixion in love for mankind. "I have a baptism to undergo, and how distressed I am until it be accomplished!" (Luke 12:50). What He accomplished was the cross. The baptism of redemptive suffering for another is fire. It is when a heart suffers unjustly while loving the attacker that love turns to fire. That kind of fire melts stone to lava—isn't it striking that it takes mountains of pressure to produce fire and molten rock!

HEARTS OF STONE IN ACTION

Sam cannot understand what his wife is talking about. He brings home the bacon. He never goes out with the fellows, never drinks, never swears, never hits her, and goes to church with her regularly, but she is miserable. He does not know that he does all these things only by duty, like a robot.

When he kisses her, which is seldom, it is because duty and unmistakable signals demand it. For Lucy, living with him is like continually knocking on the door of an empty house. Each time she steps in and calls out, "Anybody home?" she hears only echoes. There's rarely anybody home in Sam's inner house! Neither of them can understand. On the surface even to her he is such a nice guy. Sam's parents were good people. They provided well. He never lacked for things, and they were never unkind or brutal. But they never touched or held. To shield himself from pain, Sam closed his heart with inner vows not to need affectionate touch. He came into marriage with a hidden heart of stone. Sam is still a tin man. He cannot feel, meet, cherish, and be cherished. Lucy lives in a desert—nice, always nice—nevertheless still a desert.

Ann came to me (John) discouraged because depression and thoughts of suicide continually beset her. She had a good husband, healthy children, plenty of money, friends, and good things all around her. In short, Ann had "arrived." She had everything. Performing had won her a nice life. But all that blessedness was empty. There seemed no reason for sadness, and for that, guilt increased the depression. Ann couldn't feel. She never had been able to feel. Her parents were cold, principled people. She had done well in school and even yet remained artistically superior. Recently, she had tasted enough real life in a Holy Spirit–filled prayer group in her church to discover hints of life. She wanted more, but she couldn't get going, like being stuck in neutral, unable to get in gear. She had a heart of stone.

Frequently, people who have hearts of stone are like Sam and Ann. They perform well. They do for others, but they can't feel. Most often, the telling mark is that they can't let others do for them. In those who cannot do for others, the heart of stone is no longer hidden. Everyone recognizes it, and we speak of it in the vernacular, "Who, that hard-hearted so-and-so?" But in people like Sam and Ann, the heart of stone is most difficult to detect because everyone sees their actions and thinks of them as loving people. The last thing most people would suspect of them is hardness of heart.

Ministers, doctors, and lawyers most commonly are afflicted with hidden, ossified hearts. Those who were born with loving natures but were prevented from learning true give-and-take have often built strong walls to protect those naturally tender hearts.

Now, for example, that loving nature expresses itself in the family doctor in a most compassionate bedside manner. He becomes a greatly loved father-confessor to most everybody in the town. Everybody praises him. All the townsfolk and church members tell the doctor's wife what a fortunate woman she must be to have such a saintly, gentle, loving husband.

Suppressing a desire to scream, she agrees politely and rushes home to surreptitiously gulp another jigger of whiskey, hoping she can survive another day. "If only they could see him like I do!" He can't let anyone love him, especially close family members. He must minister to everyone else. All who know about her "problem" pity that saintly man stuck with that drunken wife. But they don't know; "He will not judge by what His eyes see, nor make a decision by what His ears hear" (Isa. 11:3). Hopefully, something will happen to break through. "God is not unjust so as to forget your work and the love which you have shown toward His name, in having ministered and in still ministering to the saints" (Heb. 6:10). God wants to reward His servant by setting him free.

God Himself may actually send such a person a breakdown. Perhaps when weakened, he will learn to receive. We have noted that strong, serving people (who have never learned to receive) often have long, debilitating illnesses before they die. If everyone in heaven has only learned to serve, who will receive? Or the Lord may send a true persistent friend, who will risk enough to tell him hurtful truth. "Faithful are the wounds of a friend, but deceitful are the kisses of an enemy" (Prov. 27:6). Perhaps his own inmost spirit will begin to raise questions—"The spirit of man is the lamp of the LORD, searching all the innermost parts of his being" (Prov. 20:27). Usually such questions are prompted by trials and suffering. "Stripes that wound scour away evil, and strokes reach the innermost parts" (Prov. 20:30). In some way, God will reach the heart. Our point to friends and prayer ministers is that most often such blessings will come in disguise. We need to celebrate the stern hand of God and stand by ready to pick up the pieces.

LEARNING TO MELT FROZEN HEARTS

It is better, of course, when hearts can be reached in easier ways. The heart (not just the mind) must be penetrated by logic, touch, and the Word of God—and whatever else accomplishes insight into the causes in early family life. Talk and prayers must be to that end. But from there on the struggle is not ended; it has only begun. The heart alternately receives and rejects, comes forward and retreats, embraces and attacks, storms and lapses into silence. Reverting to old ways just when everything seems to be going well need not cause dismay or discouragement. People have to be moved into life by the "kisses" of Prince Charming

(Jesus) through good friends and prayer ministers. (This does not mean physical kisses or hands inappropriately touching, but only warm, appropriately placed touches in the Lord.)

The body of Christ must not abdicate their responsibility. The person's budding life is for that time dependent on our steadfastness in loving. A person must not be handed back solely to Jesus.

Agnes Sanford, greatest of faith healers in the mid-twentieth century, came to us (John and Paula) needing love to come out of her walls of depression and live again (after the death of her husband). We couldn't believe this great saint needed us. We handed her back to the Lord in prayer. She went away crushed. She could move mountains by faith to give healing to countless others and had no faith at all to receive from God for herself! She needed God's love through human vessels. Good friends and prayer ministers must know their worth as God's messengers of love.

Sometimes Jesus will sovereignly and quickly melt a heart of stone. Testimonies of such abound. But far more frequently He chooses to do it slowly—oh, so slowly—through human vessels. Perhaps He does this to create the bonds of love in His Church. To heal hearts of stone, He calls us to be true friends. Ministering to such people is not gimmickry and not mainly prayer, but friendship. "A man of many companions may come to ruin, but there is a friend who sticks closer than a brother" (Prov. 18:24, NIV). "Two are better than one, because they have a good return for their work: If one falls down, his friend can help him up. But pity the man who falls and has no one to help him up! Also, if two lie down together, they will keep warm. But how can one keep warm alone? Though one may be overpowered, two can defend themselves. A cord of three strands is not quickly broken" (Eccles. 4:9–12, NIV).

The best oven for melting hearts is not only a single Christian counselor or prayer minister, but also a group in the church. One frozen intellectual in our church stormed in and out of fellowship regularly, but the prayer groups persistently prayed for him and met him at the door with hugs. They lightheartedly sidestepped his brilliant mind and met him with embracing spirits and bodies. Before long, he found excuses to let people know he was leaving, in order not to succeed in passing the door without being hugged half a dozen times. No way was he ready to admit what he was doing or what was happening. Eventually he received the Lord and became the warmest greeter at the door, hugging everyone.

To sum up, hearts of stone, like inner vows, lie hidden, often behind the warmest exteriors. The telling mark is an inability to receive love, often hidden behind an expressively loving exterior. Like inner vows, hearts of stone resist change. Unlike inner vows, authority alone will not melt a heart of stone. Only prayer and persistent touch will set fire and bring to life. Love becomes fire when refused or attacked yet given anyway. Rejoice and persist.

CHAPTER 8

LASTING HEALING
FROM SEXUAL ABUSE

But all things become visible when they are exposed by the light, for everything that becomes visible is light. For this reason it says, "Awake, sleeper, And arise from the dead, And Christ will shine on you."

—EPHESIANS 5:13–14

Every plant which My heavenly Father did not plant shall be rooted up.

—MATTHEW 15:13

Several years ago, John and I met a medical doctor at a seminar where we were teaching. For years she had been engaged in research concerning one of the elusive questionable-cause, no-cure terminal diseases. She was excited because at long last she had found some answers, had sufficiently validated them, and had submitted them to authorities for further scrutiny. As she talked about her work, it was revealed that she is a scientist who not only calls herself a Christian, but she also knows God well enough to listen to Him and, as in Luke 8:15, takes care how she listens.

We were intrigued as this brilliant doctor shared in a childlike manner how she has learned to submit her hunches to the Lord and has practiced hearing and weighing the guidance He has given her. Sometimes He would speak to her through the Scriptures, but sometimes directly, until she knew which alternatives to choose, what frontiers to press beyond, and what dark alleys to explore. There was an infectious joy bubbling from her in gratitude for the goodness of God, that He had blessed her so faithfully with insight to discover what had been hidden and also that He had protected her from the scorn of some colleagues who might have ridiculed her "unscientific" method had they known.

As she talked, I found myself remembering George Washington Carver, who discovered a multitude of uses for the peanut by the same sort of listening process. I wondered how many of life's mysteries and blessings remain hidden to us because we fail to listen when God is quite willing to speak. "You do not have because you do not ask" (James 4:2).

I am sure that many of the currently incurable diseases of mind, body, and spirit that plague mankind would be rendered curable were more of us to come to the point of having what Luke 8:18 suggests some of us have: "For whoever has, to him shall more be given." Whoever has what? I believe the answer to that question is "trust." If we had trust in a God who treads down all "our adversaries" (Ps. 108:13), who heals "all [our] diseases" (Ps. 103:3), who not only desires "truth in the innermost being" but will also "teach me wisdom" in the "inmost place" (Ps. 51:6, NIV), we would not have to continue to be defeated by the unknowns that now cause us to be afraid.

"All things become visible when they are exposed by the light"

(Eph. 5:13), and Jesus is that light. He speaks to us by His Holy Spirit and empowers us with the gifts of His Spirit. Inspiration comes to many as a gift from the Lord without their knowing the Giver. How much more to them who seek Him and obediently serve Him! It is time for the Church to awaken from spiritual sleep and allow the light of Christ to shine in all our inmost places to discover those things that block and to shine on all our natural talents that they may break forth to bring healing and wholeness to the body of mankind.

LET GOD MAKE IT HAPPEN

When we pray for insight and wisdom to minister, and the Lord gives us a little, we are often too timid and fearful to use that little. We say, "I don't know enough to pray." "I don't want to go around messing with somebody's insides and hurt them more than they are already."

There is truth to be heeded in both of those statements. Humility, sensitivity, and caution are always prerequisites for effective ministry. But what often underlies our reticence is, "I don't know enough to be in control, and I'm afraid to risk it. What if it doesn't work? What if I am not received? What if the flak hits the fan?" We need to understand that when we sit down to minister to one another we are not the healers. God is. We do not have to make anything happen. He will. We do not need the security of guaranteed success. He *is* the guarantee. "And He said, 'My presence shall go with you, and I will give you rest'" (Exod. 33:14).

Romans 8:28 says, "And we know that God causes all things to work together for good to those who love God, to those who are called according to His purpose." To those of us who know we are called according to His purpose but can't quite grasp the details, the Scriptures are reassuring when they say, in Ephesians 3:20, that He is able to do "exceeding abundantly beyond all that we ask or think, according to the power that works within us." Thousands of times when John and I have prayed according to the glimmer of light the Lord has given, we have been overwhelmed with surprise and gratitude for the quality of the fruit that has resulted.

Our responsibility is to listen to the Lord, respond to Him as best we can, and offer whatever He gives us as a door opener to more. Our faltering prayer may be just that which will enable a faint aroma of the Lord to flow in so that the one for whom we pray will "taste and see that the LORD is good" (Ps. 34:8) and eventually fling wide the gates "that the King of glory may come in!" (Ps. 24:9). When we have been faithful over a little, He will set us over much, and not before. And it is a comfort to know that God is bigger than our mistakes.

In the light of what has been said, I offer the following, which are simple clues too small to describe the whole of what we have seen the Lord accomplish. But they are clues that have become keys to unlock doors through which the Lord has given some miracles in our ministry and in the ministry of others.

WOUNDING CAUSED BY SEXUAL ABUSE

Our own experience in prayer ministry, confirmed by friends who have been foster parents to many abused children over the years, is that girls who have been sexually abused by fathers, stepfathers, other male relatives, or friends they trusted respond usually in two extremes: they either become very promiscuous, or they shut down their sexuality totally. Some of the reasons they behave promiscuously are:

- ❧ A sense that much of their glory, dignity, and worth is gone, so why not blow it?

- ❧ A desire to punish—to turn men on and then leave them

- ❧ A desire to prove that men are nasty and no good

- ❧ Sex has become identified with love and attention; they will endure sex to receive the affection they hunger for

The latter reason manifests itself the most frequently. In fact, the lack of a father's wholesome nurturing affection is often that which sets the stage for sexual abuse. A girl's need for love sends out signals that are misread. A man, confused about his own masculinity and unaware of his God-given role as a protector, "turns on" when he catches the "I need to be loved" signals, and then "shorts out" his conscience and sets a fire of abuse that burns and destroys.

Sexual abuse, we believe, is the most damaging of all abuse. That is because the body was built to be a temple of the Holy Spirit (1 Cor. 6:18–20), to be shared with a mate in sanctification and honor, not in lust (1 Thess. 4:3–6). As we are joined to one another in sexual embrace, it is never a physical union only; it involves our whole person. It is impossible to touch body only, because it is the spirit living in every cell that gives life to the body (James 2:26).

In the marriage relationship, we are designed to become one flesh in blessedness as God ordained (Gen. 2:24). To come together in any other way is defilement (Heb. 13:4). Woman is described as a deep well of refreshment for her man in Proverbs 5:15–19. A man who drinks from a well that is not his not only violates and uses the woman, but he also defrauds the brother who is to become her future husband (1 Thess. 4:3–6). Wholesome sexual relationship within the sanctity of marriage strengthens personal identification in the sense of being chosen and cherished, belonging and resting where God has called us to be.

Sexual abuse confuses identity, plants fear of being chosen, offers no promise of being cherished, and makes a girl wonder how God could allow such a horrible thing to happen.

TIME magazine reported:

> The majority of parents who batter their helpless children or molest them sexually or simply deprive them of sustenance do not know—or are not able to admit—that they need help. If somehow accused of maltreatment, they deny it. The few who do want aid frequently do not know where to find it. Far too often those who are asked to help do not know how to provide it. Even the experts disagree on how best to treat the offenders. Less is known, and less is done, about helping the victims.[1]

God is revealing to the Church the way of healing. He is purging our hearts and calling us to be a shelter and a refuge and protection from the storm and rain (Isa. 4:6).

> The Spirit Himself bears witness with our spirits that we are children of God.
>
> —ROMANS 8:16

It is not the will of your Father who is in heaven that one of these little ones perish.

—MATTHEW 18:14

Whoever causes one of these little ones who believe in Me to stumble, it is better for him that a heavy millstone be hung around his neck, and that he be drowned in the depth of the sea.

—MATTHEW 18:6

See that you do not despise one of these little ones, for I say to you, that their angels in heaven continually behold the face of My Father who is in heaven.

—MATTHEW 18:10

Like a shepherd He will tend His flock, in His arm He will gather the lambs, and carry them in His bosom; He will gently lead the nursing ewes.

—ISAIAH 40:11

Whoever receives one child like this in My name receives Me; and whoever receives Me does not receive Me, but Him who sent Me.

—MARK 9:37

GETTING HEALED OF THE EFFECTS OF SEXUAL ABUSE

It is clear that the Lord is intensely concerned for the sake of His children. If you were that girl who was hurt by your father, other trusted male friend or relative, or even a stranger, here are some ways you can be healed in the name of Jesus from the wounds of sexual abuse. It would be best for you as a victim to get the help of a prayer minister to help walk you through this process. If you are one who ministers to victims of sexual abuse, these suggestions will be helpful to you as well.

Lead the one who was abused to forgive the offender.

The Bible states some clear principles concerning forgiveness:

> For if you forgive men for their transgressions, your heavenly Father will also forgive you. But if you do not forgive men, then your Father will not forgive your transgressions.
>
> —MATTHEW 6:14–15

That is for the simple reason of the power of the laws of God. We read in Galatians 6:7: "Do not be deceived, God is not mocked; for whatever a man sows, this he will also reap." If we insist on sowing unforgiveness, we will inevitably reap unforgiveness.

While we want at some point to communicate to the one to whom we minister what the laws of God are, we must be careful not to use the Word as a weapon against one whose head and heart are already bloodied. It is very difficult for one who has been deeply wounded by abuse to understand that forgiveness *must* be given. It seems to the abused one that the abuser deserves to be punished. In the victim's helplessness, his hate, anger, and resentment may have seemed to be his only means of retaliation.

An effective way to begin, then, is first to empathize, then to explain that anger, hate, and resentment held in our hearts work inside us like a poisonous substance. If allowed to remain, they sicken not only our hearts, minds, and spirits, but they also affect our physical health as well because of the tension they create. "When I kept silent about my sin, my body wasted away through my groaning all day long" (Ps. 32:3). We thereby lose peace, joy, and the ability to expect and receive kindness from those who are prepared to give it, because hate is like a greedy cancer that destroys healthy body cells.

If hate is allowed to remain and grow, it will someday become out of control, and we will find ourselves hurting someone else in the same way we were hurt. At this point in prayer ministry, it is often possible to begin to talk somewhat about how his abuser would not have done what he did had he not been wounded himself. If the person to whom ministry is given can identify with the woundedness of his abuser, some basis for compassion may be laid, which more easily allows forgiveness to occur.

God will deal with those who sin against us. "Never take your own revenge, beloved, but leave room for the wrath of God, for it is written, 'Vengeance is Mine, I will repay,' says the Lord" (Rom. 12:19). Our call is simply, "Be kind to one another, tender-hearted, forgiving each other, just as God in Christ also has forgiven you" (Eph. 4:32).

Forgiveness is not easy. It is not something we can accomplish by an act of our will. But we *can choose* by an act of our will to forgive. Jesus can then accomplish the miracle of forgiveness for us. We can choose to be made willing. We probably will need to make that choice again and again; in the process the Lord Himself will cause it to become real in our hearts because we are no longer willfully hanging on to the "right" to hate.

Children are often amazingly willing to forgive because their hearts yearn so powerfully for reconciliation with their parents. The wounded child in the heart of an adult finds it more difficult. He has practiced his feelings for so long a time. Or he has suppressed them, covering them over with a façade of "forgiveness." The telling point may come when the prayer minister says, "Imagine now that you are a little child, and your parents who abused you are standing right here. Can you tell them you forgive them?" In our experience adults will often break into sobs as their real feelings come rushing to the surface. And sometimes they try to say, "I forgive," and choke on the words.

Pronounce absolution (assurance of forgiveness) to the one who was abused.

Many people resist the idea that the wounded one needs forgiveness for anything. They see him/her as an innocent victim and want only to give comfort. But the victim, no matter how much comfort may be given, may still retain *feelings* of guilt until that guilt, real and/or imagined, has been addressed in prayer. So if the abused cannot let go of false guilt, even if he knows he is not guilty, we pray, "On the basis of the Word of God, you are forgiven...I forgive you in the name of the Lord Jesus Christ."

Why the feelings of guilt? First of all, there is real guilt in terms of anger, hate, loathing, wanting to kill, perhaps even wanting to die. In such cases, it is good to quote such passages as:

> In Him we have redemption through His blood, the forgiveness of our trespasses, according to the riches of His grace, which He lavished upon us.
> —EPHESIANS 1:7–8

> If we confess our sins, He is faithful and righteous to forgive us our sins and to cleanse us from all unrighteousness.
> —1 JOHN 1:9

> As far as the east is from the west, so far has He removed our transgressions from us.
> —PSALM 103:12

Second, there is guilt that proceeds from confusion. A girl who has been sexually abused by a family member or friend knows she has done something to attract attention. But she was not looking for the kind of attention she received. She fears that there is something wrong with her that would cause such a terrible thing to be done by someone she admired and trusted.

Every girl needs to develop a sure and wholesome sense that she is beautiful, loveable, and a treasure. She learns to rest in the loveliness she was created to be as she sees the sparkle in her father's eye, as he compliments and affirms her, and as he expresses affection for her. The confidence she develops in relation to her father enables her to meet her husband and nurture him in warm relaxed freedom, knowing she is a blessing to him. This happens only if her father responds to her as admirer and *protector*, if he *shields* the beauty he sees developing and unfolding in her, if his affection is *clean* and his attention *trustworthy*. But if a girl reaches out in a normal healthy way for appreciation and fatherly affection, and her father (or any other male relative) violates the God-given beauty he was assigned to protect, she is horribly betrayed. She feels guilty for reaching out, for needing, for wanting to be thought pretty. She may unconsciously make an inner vow not to be pretty if beauty attracts nastiness. She may later neglect herself or develop a severe problem with obesity. She may make a deep inner vow to never allow herself to get into a situation of vulnerability where anything could possibly go out of control and become destructive and dirty. Later, when she marries, she may desperately want to embrace her husband fully, but then find built-in shut-off mechanisms in operation the moment he begins to approach her.

Break the power of inner vows by the authority of the Lord Jesus Christ and loose her to be fully committed to her husband.

This breaking is accomplished by a simple word of prayer, but the one who was so bound by woundedness and fear will have to walk it out. By prayer for balm to heal the wounds, love to dissipate fear, and strength to fortify her spirit, she will be equipped to exercise the necessary discipline of choosing to risk, to open her heart, to trust, and to give herself.

Loose her spirit from the one who violated her.

Her spirit needs to be loosed from the one who violated her since, as we have said, there is no physical touch without involvement of one's personal spirit, which breathes in and through the physical body, giving it life. We simply affirm that the sword of truth in the hand of the Lord Jesus is cleaving between her and her abuser, and we direct her spirit to forget whatever degree of union was made. Her mind will not forget the incident, but her memory of it will be without a hurtful shudder or a feeling of uncleanness.

If the sexual abuse was perpetuated by her father or stepfather, another feeling of guilt may have to come to the cross. Though the girl may clearly have been a victim, though she may have been terrorized by threats of what might happen to her should she tell anyone what was happening to her, she may still feel guilty that she had been in a position that rightfully belonged to her mother. Nothing short of expressed forgiveness will lift that cloud from her and reconcile her to her mother. If her mother was aware of the abuse and did not act to stop it, the girl will certainly feel doubly betrayed and abandoned.

A number of other aspects of wounding need to be ministered to in prayer before the one who has been sexually violated is healed.

Pray for cleansing.

She feels unclean. We therefore pray with vivid imagery, seeing volumes of living water washing over, in, and through her until she is "squeaky clean." Then we pray, thanking the Lord that He has made her new. We may quote the scripture, "What God has cleansed, no longer consider unholy" (Acts 11:9). We use the water image as a symbol of cleansing rather than the "blood of the Lamb" simply because it is difficult for a little child to think of being cleansed by being covered with blood. Later we might talk about what it means to be covered with the blood of Jesus, but little ones relate more easily to soap and water. Jesus is Himself the water of life.

Pray for that sense of isolation to be removed.

Sexually abused children tend to feel that they are the only ones this terrible unspeakable thing has happened to, and if anyone knew, they couldn't be accepted. The fact of your knowing, accepting them and valuing them, is the beginning of restoration, but it is good to pray also that the walls of isolation that they have built to hide their shame be melted down and that they be set free to come forth in the light and glory of the Lord.

Sexually abused boys need healing too.

Though I have used as my example a girl who is abused, the same principles of healing are to be applied to boys. Consider the case of our son Mark. At the age of five he went to spend the afternoon at a farm belonging to some family friends. We instructed Mark to stay and play in the fenced yard, but curiosity drew him to go exploring. He came to a fence and, peering over, saw six boys across a meadow by a grove of trees. He was horrified to see them circled around two who were engaged in homosexual activity. The boys saw Mark and chased him, finally knocking him down. One grabbed him in the groin and violently squeezed, causing him a great deal of pain. Some taunted him with speculations about what they would like to do to him as a "pretty little girl." Before Mark knew it, he had been molested orally by four of the boys. They told him not to tell anyone, threatening to kill his parents if he did.

In the days that followed, he seemed withdrawn and was horrified to let anyone see him exposed in the tub. But when his mother questioned him, he stoutly denied that anything was wrong. The entire memory was then stuffed into forgetfulness.

As he grew up, he partially suppressed his masculinity. After struggling with homosexual temptations (though he never allowed himself to act them out), he fought his way clear of effeminate traits that had brought wounding ridicule during his teens, and he embraced his own masculinity fully. At this point of his choosing to be the man God created him to be, the Holy Spirit caused the memory of the five-year-old to come to consciousness so he could deal with several delusory burdens that had held him in bondage.

The first part of the story demonstrates how small children can accept tremendous burdens of guilt and apply them wrongly; Mark felt inordinate guilt for leaving the fenced yard after he had been forbidden to do so. The guilt became twisted, convincing him that he had somehow caused the perverted act that had been done to him. The second part demonstrates the power of fear over a child. He believed they really would kill his parents. Therefore he chose not to tell anyone. And third, he saw that suppression of his masculinity was mainly derived from his desire to reject masculinity, if being like those boys was what it was to be male.

As the memory returned, Mark's wife, Maureen, and others were able to pray for the frightened, guilt-laden little boy, and the weight that had borne him down for years was lifted. Not only that, but also a mystery that had been heavy on the family was made light. Paula and I had made our share of mistakes, but we could never understand how they could account for the amount of struggle Mark went through.

THE CHURCH'S RESPONSIBILITY TO PREVENT CHILD ABUSE

We may never have thrown a child against a wall to stop his crying, held his hand over the burner on a hot stove to teach him a lesson, or have violated anyone sexually, but we have all participated to some degree in feelings of anger, impatience, resentment, jealousy, envy, and lust. We have the same capacity to sin as anyone else, and the adage applies, "There, but for the grace of God, go I."

Non-Christians are not the only ones guilty of child abuse. Many children who have to be placed in foster homes come from Christian families in which parents have been caught in a performance-oriented religious spirit, interpreting the faith legalistically and trying too hard. When the children rebelled, their parents' image of themselves as good parents was threatened. In a frantic attempt to control a situation that seemed to be getting out of hand, they turned from discipline to abusive punishment.

In some cases the children's behavior triggered hidden areas in the parents they could not stand to have revealed, attributes they hated in themselves as children, for instance, but never forgave. They then projected their angers and frustrations toward self onto their children, punishing their own sin there. Many times we have been called to minister to fathers who call themselves born-again Christians who nevertheless have regularly sexually abused their daughters.

First Corinthians 12:26–27 says that if we are Christ's body, and individually members of it, then if one member suffers, we all suffer. We pray then, not only that "they" be forgiven, but also that "we" be forgiven because "we" are a part of "them." Here are some things below that we can do to appropriate healing for the abuser.

Repent on behalf of those who are abusers.

We need to repent of our sins of omission in not being sensitive soon enough to the stressful condition of others, which continued and compounded to the point of violence.

Repenting as one with other members in the body does not do away with any individual's need to repent of one's own sins. But it certainly removes the "pointing of the finger, and speaking wickedness" (Isa. 58:9) from our own hearts so we may be freer to minister in power to be a "repairer of the breach" (Isa. 58:12).

When the Lord indicates that it is appropriate, we find it effective to express our repentance verbally in the presence of the one who is wounded. If the parents of an abused child have been unable to ask forgiveness, it is some comfort for the child to hear those words expressed sincerely by a parent. Abusive parents may experience intense guilt, pain, and horror for what they have inflicted, so much so that they may enter into delusion, denying that they have abused their child or even feeling that someone else has done what they themselves actually have done. But they will not be able to come to real repentance, meaning change, until their own woundedness has been healed and their bitterness repented of. Until parents have dealt with their problem of abuse and demonstrated that healing has been accomplished, separation from their children is necessary, however hurtful.

Call to death our own attitudes of condemnation.

We are horrified when we encounter the effects of violence, especially when it has been done to children. Our natural response is to rise up in righteous anger to see to it that the guilty ones receive what they deserve. We need then to remember that those who abuse were once abused or were in some other fashion seriously wounded. They must be held accountable to the laws of our land as surely as they will be by the law of God. "So then each one of us shall give account of himself to God" (Rom. 14:12). But the attitude of our calling one another to account must be tempered by compassion and mercy.

> And so, as those who have been chosen of God, holy and beloved, put on a heart of compassion, kindness, humility, gentleness and patience; bearing with one another, and forgiving each other, whoever has a complaint against anyone; just as the Lord forgave you, so also should you.
>
> —Colossians 3:12–13

Forgiveness does not mean that we say to the guilty one, "What you did was all right." It does not mean that we should make excuses for the offender or that we should deal softly with him. It does mean that insofar as it is possible we should have the mind of Christ. At the same time as we may be called morally and legally to be part of determining and executing judgment against an offender, we must also grieve for him in love even as our Lord does. What we do in relation to him must be for his good because we care about him. If our hearts are not free from hatred and condemnation, we will be unable to identify with the abuser, who needs healing ministry as desperately as the abused. And, if our own hearts are not clear of judgment and condemnation, we will communicate destructive attitudes and compound negative emotions in the one who has been abused, blocking his healing.

Minister to the abuser.

The causal roots of the abuser's behavior must be found and healed, not by himself but through the counsel of prayer ministers. He must sincerely and completely forgive those who wounded him. As he repents of the violence he himself has committed, he needs assurance of forgiveness and the grace of the Lord to enable him to forgive himself. Beyond that he will need the supportive love of friends until he is restored in the eyes of the family and to those segments of society who know about his sin. A fuller treatment of this issue requires more space than we have here. See Paula's book *Healing Victims of Sexual Abuse*, in which there is an entire chapter entitled "Profile of an Abuser." It should also be noted that this is not an issue that should be tackled by everyday lay people. Experts in this field should be consulted and referred to.

CHAPTER 9

ANOREXIA
AND BULIMIA

...holding fast the word of life, so that in the day of Christ
I may have cause to glory.

—PHILIPPIANS 2:16

O ngoing patterns of sin and dysfunction can arise from roots of bitterness and inner vows. Even genetically based problems can be exacerbated by the turmoil such roots can cause. In the three previous books in this series of four, we have already covered how bitter roots can create, or at least contribute to, a host of maladies. After laying down a basic understanding of the building blocks of inner healing, each book has applied this knowledge to a number of personal problems. *Transforming the Inner Man* discusses performance orientation (having to do everything right to earn acceptance), the causes and effects of cult involvement, and the effects of living in a sin-sickened culture. *God's Power to Change* speaks of the slumbering spirit (a state in which one's spirit is not awakened to life); spiritual imprisonment (a state in which one's spirit, though awake, is

incapable of fully connecting with life); depression; "defilements";
demons; death wishes; shrikism (the tendency to vaunt one's righteousness by denigrating others); the effects of occult involvement; spiritual adultery (that is, the steps that can lead up to actual
adultery); and grief, frustration, and loss. *Letting Go of Your Past*
talks about marriage issues, finding a mate, gender identity issues,
problems with burden bearing (sensing and carrying others' feelings), and fitting into the body of Christ. For discussions of those
subjects, we suggest you read those books.

There are many other issues we could cover if we had the time.
For the purposes of this book, there are two closing childhood
disorders that we would like to discuss: anorexia and dyslexia.
Dyslexia is more related to prenatal issues than are most problems; anorexia (along with its cousin bulimia) is an unfortunate
problem that is being said to affect more and more children
at younger ages. We thought it deserves our attention and is
important enough to be given space before we close the series,
especially since so many people are succumbing to this poten-
tially deadly issue.

The Loneliness of Anorexia

In August 1983, an article written by a young reporter for the *Arizona
Republic* in Phoenix, Arizona, was sent to us. It read in part:

> Death is my constant companion. Slowly, day by day, I am
> killing myself, and though overwhelmed by fear, I seem power-
> less...I have anorexia and bulimia...At times I starve myself.
> Other times I gorge myself with food, then purge my body of
> its life-giving nutrients. I am being treated for these disorders,
> but so far with little success....How I hate myself for what I

have become. I want to live, to let life fulfill its many promises, but this problem I have—these illnesses I know can be fatal—have taken over. They seem to be more powerful than my fear, stronger than my desire for life...I am ashamed...my family is unaware...I have avoided developing friendships with my co-workers for fear they would discover my embarrassing secret...I can't stand to be alone...I'm also afraid of being with other people.

The reporter went on to describe the guilt, self-loathing, emptiness, and periods of deep depression she was suffering. Therapy had not had a lasting effect. She concluded with the heartrending: "I am so lonely and afraid. How long will I continue with this?"

Many remember with great sorrow the death of Karen Carpenter, an anorectic. We happened to be guests of friends at the Beverly Hills Hotel when she was married and watched the arrival of her wedding guests. We have enjoyed her music and have lamented the loss of one who had so much to give.

It is not a hard thing to handle the heart tugs we feel for the pathos of strangers who seem unreal because they are far removed from us. It becomes more difficult to be detached when people call on the phone asking for help, even though it is nearly impossible to do much more than soothe problems long distance in short doses. But when the Lord places His hurting children on our doorsteps and places a burden in our hearts for them, we know we are involved, and we reach out then for answers only God can give.

Annette manifested symptoms common to anorectics: significant weight loss, confusion about the seriousness of that symptom (she feared being fat), irregular and suppressed menstrual periods, insatiable appetite, and loss of hair. There came a day when she could starve herself no longer. She began bingeing on huge amounts of sugary foods. Terrified that she might gain weight, she would then throw it all up. Anorexia had given way to bulimia. She suffered periodic depression that seemed to have less to do with concern over her ill health than it did with a basic drive for perfection and her feelings that she was incapable and worthless. Guilt was overwhelming but unidentified except in terms of having gone through an extremely rebellious teenage period. She had accepted the Lord and knew she was forgiven, but she did not feel forgiven.

We looked for emotional roots. Annette's parents, though they loved her, were unable to express their affection. There was little affection given to the children or exchanged between the parents, who slept in separate bedrooms. In fact, there seemed to be little or nothing experienced corporately in the family. As she described her scant childhood memories, we received the impression of a handful of nameless people dressed in gray, sitting around in insulated compartments, with no one to call them out. In response to questions concerning her birth, she replied emphatically that she was a disappointment. She was not invited, and she should have been a boy.

Every anorectic and bulimic we have met has been extremely spiritually sensitive. Annette was no exception. She would sense these tensions around her, even when everyone hid their pain behind a smile. But she was often unable to identify what she sensed. When she did manage to articulate it, she was told she was imagining things. No one was angry. No one was hurt. Everything was fine. So Annette did what small children so often do. She believed what she was told.

But she also did what very sensitive children do. Somewhere inside, she could not let go of her perception that something was wrong somewhere. Not knowing how to remedy the situation, she came up with a single solution to two separate problems. First, how does a sensitive little girl help out floundering grown-ups? To make them happy, she tries to be perfect. But that creates a problem, for she can't be perfect. So she blames herself for whatever the unidentified problems are. And she hates herself for being different, for feeling what she thinks others don't feel and sensing what others do not sense. Second, how does such a "defective" child keep from burdening grown-ups? She simply makes herself go away. Anorexia was a way to accomplish both. It was a way to be "perfect," and it was a way to make herself go away, fulfilling a death wish.

Since Annette picked up others' feelings but couldn't identify and resolve them, she was filled with so much accumulated pain that the torment was unspeakably unbearable. When she finally succumbed to bulimia, she found the one outlet that seemed to bring relief, at least for a short while after each binge

Her father lived in his intellectual world. Occasionally he would attempt to draw her into conversation but scorned her for her inability to keep up with him intellectually. She felt lost and ashamed in his world of interests, and he never entered hers. She felt that her mother was also looked down upon. Compliments were never given, even when deserved. Annette is a beautiful girl, but she had never heard her father say, "You're pretty," or "I'm proud of you." She tried hard to please, but not feeling that she had made it, she abandoned the effort for a while with a vengeance, going to the other extreme to do all the things she knew were not pleasing, especially to her father.

When she was barely seventeen she had an abortion, and though she was pressured to do it and chose to believe counsel that it was all right, she was devastated in her heart. As time went on, she became a Christian and couldn't understand why the joy that other new Christians felt eluded her. She strove to perform as she felt a good girl should, to live up to every letter of the law. Rather than come to peace, she felt more than ever that she had failed miserably to be anything she was supposed to be. She brooded under a tyranny of feelings.

Prayer for the Anorectic

Ministry to Annette began with prayer for the healing of her wounded heart that had never felt wanted, rarely been nurtured, could never be what the people most important to her wanted even if she could perform perfectly, because she was the wrong sex in the first place. We called to death the lies that she had accepted about herself; affirmed her beauty, worth, and belonging in Father God; and called her forth in the name of Jesus to find her own place in the sun where she could thrive and grow.

In our prayer we communicated that the Lord was now trans-planting her, putting her into new soil. She was no longer in the darkness; now the light of the Lord was enfolding her. We asked the Father to hold her and let His delight be written upon her heart. Then we prayed that she be enabled to forgive and that she be forgiven. We communicated the absolute forgiveness of the Lord Jesus for her sins, in no uncertain terms, and spoke in the authority of the Lord Jesus to any voices that might tell her otherwise, "Be still, in the name of Jesus." Later we called her forth to life in prayer again and again.

Emotionally, she had never left the womb to venture into anything that was her own. She had been carried into destructive adventure by her hungers and angers and had allowed opportunists to use and abuse her. She needed repeated prayer and committed friendship from us to give her the strength and courage to walk in the new life the Lord offered her. In the process she began to gain victory over anorexia. But the final victory came with the revelation that she had never really grieved for her aborted child. It was as if she could not really choose life until she had wept for the one she had taken.

It was clear to us that Annette had been punishing herself for failing to be what she thought people wanted, for failing to be what God called her to be, but far more importantly for the guilt that she had been unable to handle. The self-punishing focused in her body. She had wished herself dead.

Annette needed gentle coaching about how to identify where others were in the wrong and how to stop blaming herself for everything around her. But most of the self-blame had been done unconsciously. For anorectics and bulimics, self-blame is not a conscious practice; it is a way of being. Their self message is not summed up by the words, "I am to blame for what others do." Rather, it is, "I *am* the bad that others feel. I, as a person, am wrong." We taught her how to take others' burdens to the cross in prayer when God called her to and how to let them go when He did not. We helped her to distinguish her feelings from those she automatically picked up from others. Most importantly, Annette needed much practice in identifying her own feelings, putting them into words, and in allowing God's comfort to permeate them so that her emotions became restful release, not a dark tumultuous dungeon.

The end of the tale and the beginning of the new is that a handsome prince came along, kissed her, married her, and, notwithstanding the inevitable struggles, they are now on their way to living happily ever after. This sounds like something out of a fairy tale. Yet it is true for the following reasons: Annette married a prince of a young man who, because of his relationship to Jesus and undying determination, is able to give her the unconditional love and consistent compassionate affirmation she needs to support her decision to choose life. More importantly, Annette made a heartfelt personal commitment to the Prince of Peace Himself. In her relationship to the Lord Jesus Christ, she is choosing to exercise the kind of daily discipline necessary to hold fast to the word of life (Phil. 2:16) and to walk as a child of light (Eph. 5:8).

With each temptation to fall back to former resentment, fear, guilt, anxiety, self-condemnation, and striving, she is learning to obey Romans 6:11–14. That meant to deny the tyranny of her feelings and offer herself to Jesus in each instance. Because the wounds, griefs, and guilts of her heart have been seen, faced, and forgiven, and the habit patterns brought to death on the cross in prayer, she is set free to grow into the abundant life promises of the Lord. Her ability to discipline herself is empowered by Him. When she begins to fail in the discipline of walking in her new life, those who love her bear her up in prayer and by gentle reminders.

Some time ago I (Paula) came across an article in the *Journal of*

Christian Healing, volume 5, number 1, which confirmed almost point by point what we have experienced with our Annettes. There R. Kenneth McAll, MD, quoted R. Gladstone saying that:

> ...in fifty cases of anorexia nervosa the most common single factor was the anorectic's devotion to the idea of perfection. Gluttony, acquisitiveness, and pleasure were cardinal sins. Guilt was to be expiated by punishing the body mass.[1]

He then reported from a lecture given by a psychiatrist named Graham at Chichester Hospital, England, 1979, that:

> ...children who feel better off dead...are afraid of further loss of communication especially after the loss of a parent through death or divorce or when a parent becomes mentally disturbed.[2]

"Divorce," said Dr. McAll, "creates more of a problem than death....In line with this thinking, anorexia can be seen as a manifestation of morbid grief."

The article went on to report a study of eighteen anorexia cases over a five-year period. All had failed to respond to hospital treatment. In the family histories of seventeen cases, there were a total of twenty-five deaths that were either by suicide or other violent causes. There were five terminations of pregnancy for nonmedical reasons and eight miscarriages. There were deaths from accidents or suicide in ten families. Abortions and miscarriages that had not been mourned were found in seven families.[3]

A ritual mourning process was prescribed for all these cases. By this we mean that a service was held at which the patient and/or his family could go through the mourning process, accept forgiveness for sins (attitude or deed), and commit the dead to God. "In this service," said Dr. McAll, "the whole purpose of the life and death of Jesus Christ is consciously shown forth for the benefit of the living and the dead." Later in his article he reported:

> In fifteen of the cases relief from anorexic symptoms followed a ritual mourning process. Three patients who followed the suggested course of action claimed to be cured within twelve months, one within a week, seven within six months, and four over a period of fourteen months. None needed readmission to a hospital. All were followed up over a period of at least one year.[4]

Dr. McAll reported that by the time his article was completed for printing, he had treated sixty-four cases in this way (through 1981). Four families refused to cooperate. In ten cases the results were not complete, but in forty-nine cases relief was sustained. According to Dr. McAll, there are at least two other doctors who had successes with similar treatment: Dr. William Wilson, professor of neuropsychiatry at Duke University, North Carolina, and Dr. Raimbault at the Children's Hospital, Rue de Sevres, Paris.

We agree with Dr. McAll and others who say that much of the etiology of anorexia nervosa and bulimia is still a mystery. But we, like them, have experienced many cases in which these factors are present: unresolved guilt in the patient or an immediate family member, or unmourned death or loss. Usually there has been great trauma that has not been adequately faced and therefore has not been healed. Often there is a history of aborted or miscarried babies that has not been recognized and dealt with in terms of guilt or loss. And even when none of these factors are present, there is always, at least among those to whom we have ministered, a sensitive soul who cannot process her own feelings, much less the feelings she picks up from others.

In our experience we have not prescribed a funeral service as a means of helping the patient to go through the mourning process. We have pursued this effect by prayer and have shown forth "the whole purpose of the life and death of Jesus Christ... for the benefit of the living and the dead" in the process of prayer ministry. However, we applaud the ritual mourning process as valid in any case and perhaps even necessary in many.

CHAPTER 10

DYSLEXIA

Trust in the LORD with all your heart, and do not lean on your own understanding. In all your ways acknowledge Him, and He will make your paths straight. Do not be wise in your own eyes; fear the LORD and turn away from evil. It will be healing to your body, and refreshment to your bones.

—PROVERBS 3:5–8

I t is not our purpose here, nor are we qualified, to present a scientific discussion concerning dyslexia. We do consider it valuable, however, to share with you the clues the Holy Spirit has given us that have enabled us to pray very effectively for a number of dyslexics who have come to us for help.

Those who suffer from dyslexia are often deeply wounded. First of all, their frustration level is high because of the difficulties they experience with language, especially with reading. It is hard for them to tell left from right; a *d* may look like a *b*, or a *u* like an *n*. They may confuse *p* and *q*, and *w* and *m*. Some dyslexic children write letters, words, or entire sentences backward. They may have difficulty reading, because theyfindithardtoseewordsasseparate fromoneanother. Pronunciation of words may be twisted; "bakset"

201

instead of "basket," for instance, and "aks" instead of "ask." They have difficulty with math for the same reason. The symbols do not appear to them as they do to others.

Dyslexics are confused about time and space dimensions: up and down, yesterday and tomorrow. Many cannot tell left from right. We have observed that they have difficulty sensing the passing of time. One six-year-old child had to be watched to insure that he arrived at school on time because he could lose himself in the game of kicking dry leaves, not realizing that literally hours were passing. We have seen a number of dyslexic children and teenagers who expressed sincere intention to follow a schedule but responded to some disruptive stimulus that drew them off course, then to another, and another, which totally fractured intended plans and purposes. Later they could not account for the loss of time.

The second wounding comes in terms of the expressed frustration of others who do not recognize or understand the problems of dyslexics. Parents and teachers often pressure such children to learn and perform as if it were simply a matter of choice. Ridicule is often piled on them by teachers and fellow students. Hurtful forms of discipline to make them pay attention are often applied. One third grader was continually thumped on the head by his teacher because his attention wandered; he would lose his place in reading and stumble in his efforts. The other children in the class found this punishment a source of merriment and laughed mercilessly. That same dyslexic child had difficulty in physical education because of his space disorientation (he could not aim or catch), and the teacher belittled him day after day in the presence of the class, calling him "Suzie" and "Pansy."

It is not surprising that a dyslexic child often becomes withdrawn and hostile if his problem is not diagnosed and treated. Many become dropouts and juvenile offenders. Almost always they suffer tremendous feelings of loneliness because of the isolation effected by misunderstanding and emotional abuse. It might be comforting to some to know that there are many famous people who were dyslexic, among them Albert Einstein, Thomas Edison, Leonardo da Vinci, George Patton, Woodrow Wilson, Nelson Rockefeller, and Olympic gold medalist Bruce Jenner.[1]

Obviously dyslexia has nothing to do with lack of intelligence or ability, as these lives testify. The child I described in the above paragraph went on to earn his master's degree and is presently an extremely gifted artist by avocation and counselor by vocation. The Lord has healed his dyslexia and is not only *healing* his wounded spirit, but also is *transforming* that to be part of the very essence of his sensitivity to others in his ability to do prayer ministry excellently.

How Do We Pray for a Dyslexic?

We first sought the Lord about this some thirty years ago when we were speaking at a church in Ohio. A despairing mother brought her ten-year-old son to us. We questioned as we usually do concerning family history. I don't remember the details, only that there were elements of his not being wholly welcomed in the family. The Lord clearly spoke to our hearts a message that startled and puzzled us: "Because of emotionally painful circumstances surrounding his birth, he didn't want to be born. His spirit is in his body backward." That was probably a symbolic description of the way his spirit was turned away from life. To think of being in the body backward even violates our understanding of the relation of spirit and body. But we prayed obediently as the Lord led, first that he be forgiven his rebellion against the life that God had created for him to live. We asked if he would forgive those who had wounded him by rejection at his conception and by ridicule and impatience as he grew up. He consented. The Lord directed us, "I want you to see Me by vision reaching in and turning his spirit around (again, probably symbolically) to face forward in life, and then to heal his coordination." We prayed obediently, and then we asked the Lord to integrate every part of his being into a harmony. We instructed the boy to make a daily discipline of saying, "I choose life."

The next day we received an excited call from his mother who informed us that his teacher had called to say that somehow suddenly the boy could read and that the school was advancing him two grade levels.

Healing is not always that quick. More often improvements manifest themselves steadily over a period of time. But consistently we have observed the same general conditions in those suffering from forms of dyslexia:

1. Woundedness in the spirit dating back to conception and/or infancy

2. Fear, anger, fleeing back from and rejecting life

3. Resultant breaking of inner harmony and a physical manifestation of the scrambling of the inner being

We have prayed, using as basic ingredients:

1.   Healing for the wounded spirit

2.   Forgiveness for rebellious fleeing back

3.   Prayer for ability to forgive those both in the past and present who wounded

4.   Prayer describing the Lord reaching in and "turning the spirit around" to face forward and to be integrated and coordinated with every other part of the person

5.   Prayer for healing of the part of the brain involved in dyslexia

6.   Prayer to empower the person to choose life

After inner healing is done, the process of healing continues in terms of:

1.   Healing relationships that were strained during the years of struggles with learning

2.   Acquiring written-language skills if the person was unable to develop them earlier

3.   Breaking old habits and building in new disciplines

It is well known that dyslexia has a genetic component, so spiritual rebellion alone cannot cause it. However, even genetic conditions can be greatly exacerbated by bitter-root issues. It appears to us that many dyslexics have a long-standing disagreement with life, which for many might have begun as early as the womb. Some felt rejected before birth. Others were conceived in a time of turmoil or at an inconvenient time. Still others were nearly miscarried or aborted. Or perhaps something happened in infancy that made life seem undesirable. Others turned away from life because of the problems caused by the dyslexia itself. For whatever reason, they seemed unable to embrace life. One dyslexic described life this way: "It has always seemed like I'm driving through life facing backward, watching the past recede, but never really experiencing life as it comes." Even those who reject life but are not dyslexic can relate to this description. But for dyslexics, it is far worse. For them, not only is the heart disoriented; the brain is too.

One young man named James tells us that as a child, when he read "Dick and Jane" books, he could see the words on the page, but he didn't realize he wasn't reading them. He memorized the text by hearing others read. No one knew he couldn't read. When preparing for spelling tests, he memorized the words in order, from one to ten. Then one day his teacher changed the order on the test. He wrote the spellings in the order he memorized them, and she accused him of cheating. He was terribly embarrassed and hurt. He tried to do everything he could with the understanding he had, and he desperately wanted people to like him. When he realized he couldn't read, he continued to try to learn, but he could only recognize individual words, one at a time. The words seemed unrelated to each other. He couldn't understand the structure and could not put them into understandable order.

At times, James stayed after school to try to explain to his teacher that he wasn't stupid, but nothing he said helped her understand. He tried to convince himself he wasn't slow. (Later in his school years, he had himself tested three times to confirm that he was, in fact, very intelligent.) Finally, James's fourth grade teacher caught on and had him tested for dyslexia. Tests confirmed it, but in his presence, two specialists said he would never be able to read beyond a third-grade level, never drive a car, never be well coordinated, and never take care of himself independently. James plummeted into a deep gray fog.

It didn't make it easier that his sister always seemed to get everything right while he was failing. His mom would give them both lists of things to do. His sister could follow the outline easily. But he would become distracted after the first chore and sail off to do other things. His mom didn't understand James, to say the least. She later berated herself for not understanding that for his condition he needed to be given one assignment at a time.

By junior high, James had learned to fake his way through classes, until he had to work in a group. The teacher made fun of his reading and writing. He learned to cope with the humiliation by becoming the class clown. No one knew James was hurting inside. In high school, most teachers were more sensitive, allowing him to take oral exams. But one teacher often yelled at him, "You're just lazy and trying to buck the system!"

James's mechanical ability was his saving grace. At eleven, he built his first car, a 1953 Ford Crown Victoria. It was easy and gave him a sense of worth. Since his dad liked working on cars, this gave James a way to connect with him. Later, James joined an auto club and got into street racing. When he was little, neighborhood kids would bring their bikes and toys to him to repair. When he was older, they brought their cars. James felt better about himself, but if he failed to please others, he would fall back into believing he was stupid and would pout. He told us, "I found a strange sort of comfort in returning to my familiar fog."

At the same time, he felt pressure from his family to go into business or some other "highly regarded" occupation. He felt looked down upon as a "grease monkey." As a teenager, he couldn't understand why his mom would be frustrated when she would arrive home from work and find a cluttered driveway. To James, that "clutter" was no mess; it was life!

After graduation, James met John and me at our son Loren's church and decided to ask us for help. The Lord directed us to pray about James's womb experience. He was born breech. In those days, fathers were not allowed in the delivery room, so his mom handled the pain and panic of a very long, difficult labor alone. The Demerol she was given to relax her actually made her extremely ill.

We prayed that God would lift away residual fears and tensions James must have felt at that time and meet him in that deep place inside where he had always wanted to flee away from life into the fog. James repented for fleeing into himself, and he agreed to embrace life. We prayed that God would reintegrate and coordinate all the parts of his brain that malfunctioned and harmonize every scattered part of heart and mind, and that James would be empowered to fulfill his determination to live life in the here and now. As dyslexics often do when we pray for them, James felt like he was spinning inside. It was as if God was turning him around to face into life, instead of away from it, and the quick change was momentarily disorienting. After the prayer, the air seemed clearer to James. Instead of a mental fog, there seemed to be a light haze, a kind of white fog James could almost see through. Life was beautiful. James felt connected. In the coming days, the "fog" continued to clear.

A week later, for the first time, James could tell his right hand from his left! His racing mind slowed to a stop. He could begin to focus and categorize thoughts. At that time, he was working at an auto parts store. One day James briefly reverted to his former ways. As he was working at the cash register, he suddenly lost all memory of how to operate it! He crossed the room to do something he knew how to do, and then his memory returned and he was able to return to the cash register and follow through. At long last, James felt able to get himself back on track.

For nearly a year, we met with James and continued to pray about other issues that fed his former disdain for life. We talked and prayed about his self-destructive patterns, especially his "I can't" attitude and all the memories and resultant bitter roots that fed it. We prayed that his spirit would be strengthened to continue to take hold of life and walk forward.

Often, such prayers caused James to momentarily feel like a gyroscope. He would lose his equilibrium, then become reoriented toward life again in some area of his heart that had been turned away from it. We prayed about the clutter and disorganization in his mind as more and more freedom, peace, and order settled in.

James decided to test his healing. He signed up for courses at

North Idaho College in Coeur d' Alene, Idaho. An understanding history teacher encouraged him, and the kid who should never have made it beyond a fourth-grade reading level made an A in a college-level course! James went on to the University of Idaho for a year and lived in the dorm, practicing how to organize his life. It was a struggle, but James managed to pull his surroundings together and earned Bs and Cs. He went on to automotive school at Spokane Community College, where he won three awards for outstanding achievement! He also won a silver medal in automotive diagnostic procedure, and in his other college courses he won two gold medals in job interview, two more in prepared speech, and two silver medals in extemporaneous speech. He was involved in designing and constructing a show car for the school. Later, he was the mechanic for a car dealership in Spokane and traveled with its owner to races all over the Northwest. James was certified a master technician and graduated with a GPA of 3.58. In his first year out of school, he became the head mechanic at a reputable business in Spokane.

We have prayed over many dyslexics, with varying degrees of healing for the dyslexia itself. The degree of healing appears to depend upon how ready the person is to embrace life. For some who have had not yet dealt with the ways they have disconnected from life, we have seen no immediate healing. For others who have dealt with it to some extent, we have seen a moderate amount of healing. And for some who have dealt with enough bitter roots to enable them to fully embrace life on every level of their being, overnight miracles have happened, such as advancing two grade levels within a few days or instantly typing twice as many words per minute.

How was a genetically based brain malfunction eliminated through inner healing? One would think that inner healing could only heal the soul, not the body. But we must remember that the body and soul are intertwined. What we do to one affects the other. If we heal the soul through inner healing, making it ready to receive life, the body is put in a better position to receive life through physical healing.

> A tranquil heart is life to the body, but passion is rottenness to the bones.
>
> —PROVERBS 14:30

CONCLUSION

"A s the twig is bent, so grows the tree." Before the advent of white men, my (John) Osage ancestors used to mark trees as signposts for trails. They would find a sapling along the way and bend up two opposite lower branches, tying them up to the main trunk at the top. The result gave the young tree the appearance of a lyre.

The tree might grow to become a ponderous giant. But it always retained that shape and thus could be depended upon for all its life to guide those with training and eyes to see.

What a parable that is for Christians! Good parenting shapes our limbs of character to become guideposts for many along the trails of life. What happens in our formative years can train into us positive patterns, from which, without grace, we may unfortunately depart. Or our reactions to traumatic woundings can form in us negative patterns from which, without grace, we do not depart. Our responses ossify into practiced habits either for good or harmful ways. This is why Colossians 3:9 says, "Do not lie to one another, since you have laid aside the old self *with its evil practices*" (emphasis added). The word *practice* in the Greek, *praxis*, is more than a mere deed. It is an action in progress, truly a *practiced* way of doing things.[1] On the good side, it is this truth that Proverbs 22:6 declares, "Train up a child in the way he should go, even *when he is old he will not depart from it*" (emphasis added). What is built into us, or what we build in reaction to the builders, stays with us, like those trees alongside the trail.

Our reactions to what happens while we are in utero, or in earliest years, on up through childhood into adulthood form who we are. Whatever is malformed must find death on the cross and transformation by the Holy Spirit, or we do not become the blessedness God intended at our creation. On the other side, whatever was formed in us in righteousness needs also to die on the cross and be restored to us, that our righteousness may not be by our flesh or parental training but by the power of the Holy Spirit in our lives—daily.

That transformation is what this book has been about. That is our intention in writing. Hopefully you have been entertained and instructed, but if it ends there, God's purposes and ours have not been fulfilled.

Somehow, we have too often become content with the first meager fruits of our initial born-again experience, as though that were all there is to growing up in Christ, or as though our conversion experience had transformed our entire nature, whereas in fact it only began the process.

In sum, let us first emphasize that our hope in this book is not only to equip the body for ministry so that we all might grow up in Christ, though that is a mighty cause for celebration when that happens. It is not merely to do a healing work, to undo harm and replace with glory, though that too would be glorious. It is not just to deal with the negative and transform to the positive. Our hope, in case you missed it, has also been to teach how to parent. If the twig is bent properly from the beginning, it can stand as a guidepost to wholesome righteous ways—and continue to stand, whatever the winds of stress and however large the storms of distress.

Along the way, we have also been talking about priorities in life. Early on the Lord said in His still, small voice (as we have reported in other books), "John and Paula, I have called you to be forerunners in the raising of the prophetic office today, pioneers in inner healing, leaders in the rediscovery of burden-bearing intercessory prayer, and incessant workers for unity in the body of Christ. But none of those tasks, and not all of them together, are not as important as the raising of your six children. They are your first task and priority in life."

God went on to teach us that we have a saying that is not altogether true. He said, "You say that you can't take it with you into heaven. But," He added, "that's only true of your material possessions. You can't take your car, your house, or your bank account into heaven with you. But you do take into heaven with you everything that you have become. You take into heaven with you everything you have learned, all the teachings about who I am, all the understandings and wisdom gained from the Bible, all the character changes that have transformed you through the years." He went on to say that if a man were to become the president of his country, or to write a great novel, or discover something that would bless millions, and so on, all those things will crumble away in the dust of history. But if a man has only one child, everything he teaches his child and every aspect of good character he has built into him will last forever! He said to us, "The raising of your children is the one truly eternal work you will do in all your life, no matter what great works you accomplish for Me!"

He explained to us that for parents, this is a primary application of what Paul wrote in 1 Corinthians 3:12–15, "Now if any man builds upon the foundation with gold, silver, precious stones, wood, hay, straw, each man's work will become evident; for the day will show it, because it is to be revealed with fire; and the fire itself will test the quality of each man's work. If any man's work which he has built upon it remains, he shall receive a reward; if any man's work is burned up, he shall suffer loss; but he himself shall be saved, yet so as through fire." He led us to understand that whatever we teach our children of the nature of God and of His wisdom is gold, whatever of true biblical knowledge of Him is silver. Precious stones are whatever is built into them of solid righteous Christian character.

From this, we saw that life tests each man's work. If our adult children stand under fire, are tested, and prove righteous by their choices and actions, that is our reward. If our adult children fail to be moral or to act in love toward others, whatever we have taught or modeled will have to be burned out of his/her life, and we have no reward. Wood, hay, and straw stand for false teachings, immorality modeled, impious behaviors, pornography in the home, cursing, drinking, speaking critically of others, and so on. Righteous character must be more than taught. It is "caught" as parents live it. Faulty character models unrighteousness into children's lives.

Each chapter in this book has been an attempt to reveal both what malforms and must die on the cross and be transformed, and what truly builds strong character for eternity. Paula and I are so grateful that so early in our parenting He drilled this lesson of priorities into us and taught us so carefully what trains and what builds character into children for eternity. We often failed to live with the children what He taught us as first priority, but we did try to remember to keep our children first. Today we are proud to the point of shedding tears of gratitude as we see our children all standing for the Lord. Each has been tested by hurts and persecutions, and each has stood, trying to manifest only the character of our Lord Jesus Christ, His love, and His gracious way of life in every circumstance. Our children are our first and best reward.

We plead with every parent or would-be parent to set your priorities straight. Do not sacrifice your children on the altar of the mammon good life, or to ambition, or even to high service to the Lord.

All the way through the Old Testament, God's servants made this mistake of failing with their children. Eli's sons, Hophni and Phinehas, sinned grievously, and he only rebuked and did not restrain them, as we see in 1 Samuel 2, especially verse 23. Both were slain in one day, and Eli fell over backward and broke his neck and died (1 Sam. 4:18). For this reason Samuel was raised to succeed Eli. But later on, God replaced the rule of the judges with a king because Samuel himself also failed with his sons: "Then all the elders of Israel gathered together and came to Samuel at Ramah; and they said to him, 'Behold, you have grown old, and your sons do not walk in your ways. Now appoint a king for us to judge us like all the nations'" (1 Sam. 8:4–5). King David's sons fell into horrible sins—Amnon raped his sister Tamar (2 Sam. 13:1–19). Absalom revolted and tried to usurp his father's kingdom (2 Sam. 15:1).

Confidentiality prevents my reporting how many preachers' children and missionaries' kids have come to us in deep moral, emotional, and spiritual trouble because their parents did not hear this lesson of priorities. Their childhood had been sacrificed to ministry. Please hear this: God did not ask the parents to make that sacrifice. Misguided zeal and the flesh did it, not God.

There are those who justify this on the basis of Mark 10:29–30: "'I tell you the truth,' Jesus replied, 'no one who has left home or brothers or sisters or mother or father or *children* or fields for me and the gospel will fail to receive a hundred times as much in the present age (homes, brothers, sisters, mothers, children and fields—and with them, persecutions) and in the age to come, eternal life'" (NIV, emphasis added). Jesus uttered these words in answer to Peter's statement, "We have *left* everything to follow you" (v. 28, NIV, emphasis added).

But does this mean *physically* leaving children? Jesus spoke of another type of "leaving": "For this cause a man shall *leave* his father and mother, and the two shall become one flesh" (vv. 7–8, emphasis added). Yet in those days, a couple typically moved into an apartment the groom and his father had built adjacent to his father's home. When Jesus said, "A man shall leave his father and mother," He did not abolish this custom. Rather, He affirmed it by announcing plans to do the same with His own bride: "In My Father's house are many dwelling places; if it were not so, I would have told you, for I go to prepare a place for you" (John 14:2). Thus, a husband was to "leave" his father, not necessarily physically, but by cutting free from demands that would draw him back into a parent/child relationship and interfere with cleaving to his wife.

In the same way, we suspect that "leaving" children means saying no to demands that can interfere with the parents' calling. Today, that might include saying no to a plea to stay home when God calls your family to move to Thailand. Or it might include taking a public stand on a moral issue when your children accuse you of being "old fashioned." If you place children ahead of God's will, you will stand to lose the parent/child relationship you idolize: "He who does not take up his cross and follow after Me is not worthy of Me. He who has found his life shall lose it" (Matt. 10:38–39). But if, for the sake of the cross, you lay down any desire to please your children at God's expense, He may give back the relationship you have risked for His sake: "...and he who has lost his life for My sake shall find it." Perhaps this is one meaning of receiving "a hundred times as much in the present age (homes, brothers, sisters, mothers, *children* and fields—and with them, persecutions)" (Mark 10:30, NIV, emphasis added). Whatever the case may be, Jesus did not mean that you should leave your children to fend for themselves while you work long hours into the evening.

First Corinthians 9:5 (NIV) says, "Don't we have the right to take a believing wife along with us, as do the other apostles and the Lord's brothers and Cephas [Peter]?" If the disciples had the right to take their wives on their travels, it would seem logical that those wives might have taken along their underage children whenever possible. On the other hand, given the dangers of travel, it would be understandable if they did not. In 2 Corinthians 11:25–27, Paul describes some of the dangers, including cold, lack of food, rivers, robbers and shipwreck. So dangerous was travel that before a trip, a traveler would pay his debts, provide for his family, give gifts to friends, and return all borrowed items.[2] It may very well have been entirely unfeasible to take the kids along. Such is rarely the case today.

But even if the disciples did physically leave their children, they would not have consigned them to a life of neglect. They would have left them in the permanent care of loved ones who served as *full-time* parents. Some mom and some dad would have been continually there for them. This is not the case with the local pastor or ministry leader who, while supposedly raising his own children, throws crumbs to them after serving banquets to his ministry.

Perhaps Jesus's words open up the possibility that in exceptionally (and we mean *exceptionally*) rare cases, God may call a select few to leave children in the permanent care of others. If that is so, God will shield the children's hearts from wounding and resentment. But if you feel called this way, be very sure of it! For if you are wrong, your children will pay the lifelong price for your foolishness. For the vast (and we mean *vast*) majority who do not receive these marching orders, there is no such thing as part-time parenting. Like ministry, parenting is a calling. You must fulfill it.

If you do not heed these words, you will still be saved, as Paul said, and will be rewarded for your service. But that highest level of reward, your children's testimony in this life and in heaven, even if great, will not be accounted to you. Others will have had to fill the void. You will have lost the reward of your children's eternal value, the greatest that can be.

Can we see in these pages the calling of God to raise our children in "the nurture and admonition of the Lord" (Eph. 6:4, KJV)?

My advice? Go back. Reread these pages with your children's welfare in mind—or grandchildren or children-to-be, as the case may be. See the teachings about how children react in the womb to who we are and what we do. Repent...aloud with the children if possible. Think through all that happened in nursing and toddler times, comprehending, perhaps for the first time, how all of your actions, or lack thereof, affected your children. Give thanks for what God managed to do rightly for your children, but see and repent for whatever God knows of your lack and adverse actions.

Get some good books on child raising and study them. Of course we recommend especially our own book *Restoring the Christian Family*. Somehow in the warped working out of history, we have managed to require assiduous study and difficult tests before we will let a man be a doctor or lawyer or any other profession, but as we said earlier, we let our people become parents—the most valuable profession on the planet—with little or no preparation.

Even when some of Jacob's sons were in their forties and fifties, he blessed them and called them into their destinies (Gen. 49). It's not too late. However old the children, it's not too late.

NOTES

CHAPTER 1
LIFE BEGINS IN THE WOMB

1. Thomas Verny, MD, *The Secret Life of the Unborn Child* (New York: Dell, 1982).

2. "An Open Window for the World," http://www.makewayforbaby.com/research.htm (accessed December 27, 2007).

3. Denise Riggs, "Early Childhood Music," as quoted in *Growing Up Magazine*, February 2006, http://www.prenatalmusic.net/article3.htm (accessed December 28, 2007).

4. Ibid.

5. Clifford Olds, "A Sound Start in Life," *Pre- and Peri-Natal Psychology Journal* 1 (1986): 82–85; Donald J. Shetler, "The Inquiry into Prenatal Musical Experience: A Report of the Eastman Projects, 1980-1987," *Pre- and Peri-Natal Psychology Journal* 3 (1989): 171–189; and Michael Clements, "Observations on Certain Aspects of Neonatal Behavior in Response to Auditory Stimuli," Paper presented at the 5th International Congress of Psychosomatic Obstetrics and Gynecology, Rome, 1977; referenced in Stephen M. Maret, PhD, *Frank Lake's Maternal-Fetal Distress Syndrome: An Analysis,* http://www.primal-page.com/mf3-5.htm (accessed December 13, 2007).

6. BébéSounds.com, "Prenatal Stimulation Helps You Have a Smarter Baby," http://www.bebesounds.com/pdfs/PrenatalStimulation.pdf (accessed December 13, 2007).

7. Verny, *The Secret Life of the Unborn Child*, 49–50.

8. Michael Lieberman, "Smoking and the Fetus," *American Journal of Obstetrics* (August 5, 1970).

CHAPTER 2
OVERCOMING WOUNDS FROM PRENATAL
REJECTION AND BIRTHING TRAUMA

1. Editorial staff, "Separating the Idea of Abortion From Killing…," *California Medicine* 113, No. 3 (September 1970): 67–68, emphasis added; as viewed at http://www.freerepublic.com/forum/a3960d7062e86.htm (accessed December 13, 2007).

2. Jeffrey Hensley, *The Zero People: Essays on Life* (Ann Arbor, MI: Servant Books, 1983), 128.

3. Ibid., 125.

4. The Center for Bio-Ethical Reform, "Abortion Facts," http://abortionno .org/Resources/fastfacts.html (accessed January 2, 2008).

5. Children and Families Subcommittee: Hearing on Teen and Young Adult Suicide, "Statement of the Honorable David Satcher, MD, PhD, United States Surgeon General," September 7, 2001, http://www.senate.gov/~dodd/ press/Speeches/107_01/0907-w1.htm (accessed December 13, 2007).

6. AfterAbortion.org, "Abortion May Increase Women's Mortality Rate: New Study Shows Women's Death Rate Following Abortion Much Higher Than Previously Known," Elliott Institute, http://www.afterabortion.org/ news/deaths_smj.html (accessed January 3, 2008).

7. Ibid.

CHAPTER 6
BREAKING CHILDHOOD INNER VOWS

1. W. E. Vine, *Vine's Expository Dictionary of New Testament Words* (Iowa Falls, IA: n.d.), 1154.

2. National Alert Registry, "Statistics on Child Molestation," http://www .registeredoffenderslist.org/blog/sex-offenders/child-molestation-statistics/ (accessed January 7, 2008).

Chapter 7
A Heart of Stone for a Heart of Flesh

1. William Wordsworth, "Ode: Intimations of Immortality From Recollections of Early Childhood," lines 59–77, http://www.bartleby .com/101/536.html (emphasis added) (accessed November 6, 2007).

2. Martin Buber, *I and Thou* (New York: Scribner's, 1958).

3. *Macbeth*, 1.5. Reference provided by Massachusetts Institute of Technology, "The Complete Works of William Shakespeare," http://shake-speare.mit.edu/macbeth/macbeth.1.5.html (accessed December 17, 2007).

4. Hans Christian Andersen, "The Snow Queen," Online-Literature.com, http://www.online-literature.com/hans_Christian_Andersen/972 (accessed December 17, 2007).

Chapter 8
Lasting Healing From Sexual Abuse

1. Ed Magnuson, "Child Abuse: The Ultimate Betrayal," *TIME*, September 5, 1983, http://www.time.com/time/magazine/article/0,9171,926134-2,00 .html (accessed December 17, 2007).

Chapter 9
Other Childhood Disorders (Part 1): Anorexia

1. R. Kenneth McAll, MD, *Journal of Christian Healing* 5, no. 1.
2. Ibid.
3. Ibid.
4. Ibid.

Chapter 10
Other Childhood Disorders (Part 2): Dyslexia

1. Dyslexia.com, "Famous People With the Gift of Dyslexia," http://www .dyslexia.com/qafame.htm (accessed December 17, 2007).

CONCLUSION

1. Vine, *Vine's Expository Dictionary of New Testament Words*, 285.

2. Fred H. Wight, *Manners and Customs of Bible Lands* (Chicago, IL: Moody Press, 1953), 270.

OTHER BOOKS BY JOHN LOREN AND PAULA SANDFORD

A Comprehensive Guide to Deliverance and Inner Healing

Awakening the Slumbering Spirit

Choosing Forgiveness

Elijah Among Us

God's Power to Change

Healing for a Woman's Emotions

Healing the Nations

Healing Victims of Sexual Abuse

Letting Go of Your Past

Prophets, Healers and the Emerging Church

Renewal of the Mind

Restoring the Christian Family

The Elijah Task

Transforming the Inner Man

Why Good People Mess Up

For further information, contact:

Elijah House, Inc.

317 N. Pines Road

Spokane Valley, WA 99206

Web site: www.elijahhouse.org

The Road to
Hope, Healing, and Spiritual Growth
Starts Here